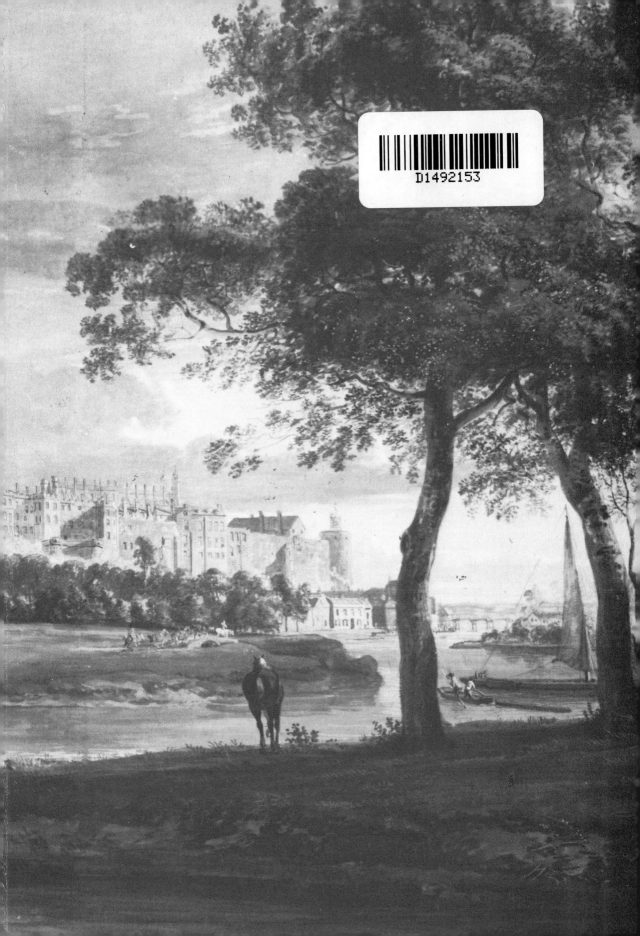

The Life and Times of
WILLIAM IV

The Life and Times of

WILLIAM IV

Anne Somerset

Introduction by Antonia Fraser

Book Club Associates London

To my mother and father

Picture research by Dee Robinson
Layout by Heather Sherratt
Series designed by Paul Watkins

Filmset by Keyspools Ltd, Golborne, Lancashire
Printed by Morrison and Gibb Ltd., Edinburgh

Contents

Introduction

WILLIAM IV succeeded to the throne of Great Britain in 1830, at a time when the monarchy was at an almost uniquely low ebb. Seven years later his geniality and good humour had at least restored it, as Anne Somerset puts it, to 'public affection' if not 'public veneration'. It was left to William's great successor Victoria to bring to that ancient institution the national respect in which it has been held ever since. Yet had the young Queen been faced with the wreckage of the monarchy bequeathed by 'Prinny', the controversial George IV, and by George III, whose long reign was punctuated by fits of madness, her task would have been infinitely harder.

At the same time William IV reigned over England during one of the most important, exciting and politically disturbed periods of her history – the years in which the Reform Bill was debated and carried through; when Whigs and Tories vied with each other for control in the new kind of Britain which was emerging, and the role of the King in supporting or negating their policies remained vital. To leave the monarchy in an improved state was therefore no easy task; nor was William himself prepared for it by his upbringing.

The third son of George III and his prolific wife Charlotte of Mecklenburg-Strelitz, William was born in 1765, five years after his father ascended the throne. Early on he was aimed for the Navy. 'I am nothing more than a sailor like yourselves' he told his new comrades exuberantly, and indeed he was to a remarkable degree stamped by the life of the quarter-deck; when he passed on to his aristocratic relations at Hanover, his rough ways and rough language shocked them. Anne Somerset paints a sympathetic – and entertaining – picture of William's years before he ascended the throne, making it clear that while debts and dissipation played their part, as so often with the Hanoverian Princes, there was much to be said for his long domestic relationship with the actress Mrs Jordan. Nelson too had a good word to say for William's qualities as a naval leader, while conceding that he had his 'foibles'.

Nevertheless the feat of 'this undistinguished old gentleman with a head shaped like a pineapple' in steering the monarchy through the shoals of the 1830s should not be underestimated. The charm of his consort Queen Adelaide, whom he married to provide an heir, having been obliged to put away Mrs Jordan, was another unlooked for asset. But in the main it was William's own geniality and accessibility, in marked contrast to the behaviour of his brother George IV, which impressed the country. Princess Lieven commented that the phrase 'happy as a King' might have been invented with William in mind.

Anne Somerset skilfully interweaves William's own story with the complicated politics of the time, introducing the many colourful – and clashing – figures of the parliamentary arena from the Duke of Wellington and Sir Robert Peel to Lord Grey and Lord John Russell (whom the King loathed for a radical).

'Well, now it must be so, and I consent.' With these words the King finally agreed, in effect, to parliamentary reform, despite the demands of the rest of the royal family that he should exercise his prerogative and block it. Wiser than them, William IV deserved the genuine popularity with his people that he had won by the time of his death.

Antonia Fraser

Acknowledgments

The publishers would like to thank the following for the loan of illustrations:

By gracious permission of Her Majesty the Queen: 14–15, 19, 52, 107–8; 10 *Robert Harding Associates*; 17, 20, 21, 23, 39, 74, 84, 86, 88, 92, 93, 117, 138, 141, 171, 177, 207 *Weidenfeld & Nicolson Archives*

By kind permission of the Greater London Council as Trustees of the Iveagh Bequest: 59

By kind permission of the Sir John Soane Museum: 126–7 *Robert Harding Associates*

By kind permission of the Viscount de l'Isle VC KG: 50

By kind permission of Brinsley Ford: 61 (photo lent by Brian Fothergill)

By kind permission of Gordon Pringle: 48

By kind permission of the Trustees of the British Museum: title page, 15 (photo Angelo Hornak); 44, 64, 70, 106, 128, 130–1 *Fotomas Index;* 133, 214–5 *Weidenfeld & Nicolson Archives*

From the Broadlands Collection: 169 *Weidenfeld & Nicolson Archives*

Photo kindly lent by Brian Fothergill: 54–5, 78

Reproduced by kind permission of Melvin Sullivan: 77

Birmingham Museum and Art Gallery: 91 *Weidenfeld & Nicolson Archives*; 178–9

Cooper Bridgeman Library: 193

Mary Evans Picture Library: 11, 22, 53, 81, 84–5, 112, 129, 134–5, 142–3, 146, 152–3, 156, 157, 165, 173, 174, 175, 210–11

Fotomas Index: 32, 98, 113, 205

Historical Picture Services: 35, 67, 75, 101, 102, 119, 121, 164

London Museum: 66, 82–3 *Weidenfeld & Nicolson Archives*

Mansell Collection: 46 *Weidenfeld & Nicolson Archives*

Monmouth Museum: 42

National Maritime Musuem: 28; 25 *Thames & Hudson Archives*; 31 *Weidenfeld & Nicolson Archives*

National Portrait Gallery: frontispiece, 45, 63, 72, 114, 116, 122, 131, 139, 148, 196–7; 13, 57, 94 (below), 95 *Weidenfeld & Nicolson Archives*; 190, 191 *Fotomas Index*

Peter Newark's Historical Pictures: 170, 175, 180, 187

George Rainbird Limited: 62 (photo Derek Witty) *Robert Harding Associates*

Royal Academy of Arts: endpapers *Weidenfeld & Nicolson Archives*

Tate Gallery: 123 *Robert Harding Associates*

Victoria & Albert Museum: 60 *Robert Harding Associates*

Weidenfeld & Nicolson Archives: 90, 94 (above), 96, 118, 120, 132–3, 159, 162, 166–7, 184, 192, 199

1
Sailor
William

ON 21 AUGUST 1765, King George III's worthy spouse Queen Charlotte was delivered at Buckingham House of her third son, subsequently christened William Henry. In 1761 the Queen had been plucked from the depths of the tiny German duchy of Mecklenburg-Strelitz to marry the young English King, thus avoiding being consigned to the aristocratic Protestant convent for which she was destined if no suitably illustrious suitor had claimed her hand. Such an establishment might well have suited her somewhat austere temperament, but although the combination of her stately reserve and innate shyness prevented her from endearing herself to high society in England no one could deny that she had settled to her wifely and regal duties with a characteristic conscientiousness. Furthermore, if she had not managed to capture the hearts of her more sophisticated subjects she had at least succeeded in securing that of the King.

The marriage had hardly begun under very favourable auspices. Before his wedding, young King George III was reputed to be enamoured of the lovely Lady Sarah Lennox, daughter of the Duke of Richmond, and Charlotte's somewhat mediocre attractions could hardly rival the radiance of this famous beauty. Nevertheless, the marriage quickly matured into a relationship of unimpeachable domesticity, a source of strength to the King in the troubled years to come and a source of surprise to the court who were accustomed to their Hanoverian monarchs mistreating their wives. An observer noted of the royal couple that they lived 'like turtle doves together, bring up their children, play music, interfere with no living soul, and yet neither foreigners nor natives care for such a gentle, shy, king, but call him "*too good*"'. In 1762 and 1763 the Queen had presented her husband with two fine baby boys, named respectively George Augustus Frederick and Frederick Augustus. After the birth of Prince William Henry, the Queen continued to demonstrate her admirable fecundity, assuring the succession with teutonic thoroughness by producing a total of fifteen children, thirteen of whom survived childhood.

Thus when William appeared in 1765 the presence of two thriving toddlers in the royal nurseries meant that there was no particular reason to suppose that he would ever be King. Horace Walpole noted of the occasion, 'If it was not for the Queen the

12

King George III, a
conscientious but
inflexibly stern father to
his large family.

peerage would be extinct; she has given us another Duke.' The
booming guns and illuminations which greeted his arrival
celebrated the safe delivery of another Prince of the blood rather
than the birth of a future monarch, and his ordered upbringing
was intended to fit him for that role rather than for the
assumption of any greater responsibility.

William's early upbringing was conducted against a back-
drop of political and social unrest. Until the access to power of
Lord North in 1770, difficulty was repeatedly found in forming
administrations whose policies were both acceptable to the

13

King and could also command a majority in Parliament. The attempt of the Government in 1768 to quash the election to Parliament of the outlawed John Wilkes resulted in violent disturbances, and throughout 1768–9 economic distress provoked the Spitalfields weavers and other craftsmen to riot periodically in London. Between 1767 and 1772 the scurrilous letters of the mysterious Junius rocked the establishment with their salacious revelations of scandal in high places. Yet these events scarcely penetrated the nurseries at Buckingham House, Richmond Lodge and Kew, between which William's early existence was divided, for little short of revolution could have disturbed the life of ordered stability that was imposed upon the royal children. They had little contact with public affairs. Admittedly, in 1769 Queen Charlotte had experimented with the custom, common in Germany, of holding an infantile drawing-room. Clad in suitably resplendent uniforms, the seven-year-old Prince of Wales and his younger brother Frederick received a succession of fawning courtiers. William and his two-year-old brother Edward co-hosted the reception, 'elegantly clothed in Roman togas'. However, subsequent cartoons so lampooned the pomposity of this junior court that Queen Charlotte was persuaded that in future her children should play a less active role at such functions. William's childhood was in consequence passed in comparative seclusion.

William's sister Princess Augusta actually asserted that she had 'been brought up in a cloister rather than a kingdom'. Presumably, however, few cloisters would be packed with such a quantity of brothers and sisters as this royal one, and certainly the regular additions to the royal nurseries ensured that William rarely lacked company as a child, and gave full scope for the exercise of his already rather boisterous high spirits. Lady Mary Coke wrote in 1770 that she had seen the royal children at play, and was much impressed by the good nature of the three-year-old Princess of Wales who was 'a good deal try'd by her brothers who pull'd her about most unreasonably'. William played rounders and cricket with his brothers and sisters and sometimes indulged in more adventurous occupations: in a letter written in July 1773 William reports that he has recently enjoyed a great deal of sailing.

One can thus hardly claim that William suffered a lonely

childhood. On the other hand, his relationship with his parents lacked a certain warmth. King George and Queen Charlotte were conscientious and dutiful parents, but they seemed incapable of cultivating any sort of cosy intimacy with their children. King George always entertained a real love for his second son, Frederick, but his deepest affections were reserved for the youngest children of his enormous brood. As for the Queen, William later asserted that he and his brother George were their mother's favourite sons. But she can hardly be accounted an indulgent mother. She rigidly adhered to the formal framework of court etiquette, even in the presence of her children, and her sons were rarely permitted to sit in her presence, a restriction which in later years made it difficult for them to have a meal in her company. Even when strolling with their parents in the gardens at Kew, the children would be formed into ordered pairs, graduated according to their size.

William did not, however, emerge as a repressed personality as a result of his somewhat constricted relations with his parents. On the contrary, the exuberant high spirits of the three eldest Princes sometimes exhausted the attendants who bore the brunt of them. In later years Mr Fairley reminisced to Fanny Burney that 'there was something in the violence of their animal spirits that would make him accept no post to live with them'. Prince William, he assured her, was especially bothersome. Yet if William sometimes appeared oppressively bumptious, his essential good nature was always evident. In August 1778 Mrs Chapone, niece of Dr Thomas, Bishop of Winchester and formerly tutor to the King, related that the King and Queen had taken five of their children to see her aged uncle: 'I was pleased with all the Princes,' she continued, 'but particularly with Prince William, who is little of his age but so sensible and engaging, that he won the Bishop's heart, to whom he particularly attached himself and would stay with him, while all the rest ran about the house.' The Prince of Wales's attentions to the old gentleman were also assiduous, if less agreeable: on leaving he pressed his hand so hard that he hurt it.

Until 1772 William was brought up in the same nursery as his eldest brothers, under the eye of Lady Charlotte Finch, a firm but fair governess. In that year, however, it was decided that George and Frederick should have their own establishment, and

opposite Prince William Henry, aged two, by Allan Ramsay.

Princess Mary, Princess
Sophia and Prince
Augustus. William's duties
at sea gave him little
opportunity to form a
close bond with his
younger brothers and
sisters. After his enlistment
in the Navy his
relationship with them
was confined to brief
periods of leave.

William and his younger brother were removed to Lord Bute's former house on Kew Green, conveniently close to the royal residence. The King selected two governors to supervise their education: General Budé, a Swiss who had acquired on his various travels an expert knowledge of the flavour of tobacco and an addiction to anchovies; and Dr John James Majendie who was later succeeded by his son, the Reverend Henry Majendie. None of them had really acquired the knack of communicating with children. William later remarked to his brother George that General Budé never truly gained his confidence, while Henry Majendie, famed among his contemporaries for the imperturbable gravity of his countenance, was hardly likely to secure the affections of the impulsive and exuberant Prince. With such tutors it was hardly surprising that William came to identify those in authority with irksome constraints rather than constructive precepts.

It was rumoured that William was displeased at being consigned to a rural existence at Kew, but his parents ignored this truculence and the Prince was forced to settle to a punctiliously regulated routine. He and his brother rose at six a.m. and at eight they trooped to the Dutch House at Kew, where they endured a strained and stiff breakfast with their parents. The morning was devoted to lessons, Prince William showing a special aptitude for mathematics. The menu at lunch was restricted to the carefully prescribed list of dishes ordained by the Queen; after the meal the children played games or worked on their model farm before a final formal visit to their parents and an early bedtime.

The Prince was not destined to endure this routine for very long. A military career was already intended for the King's beloved son Frederick, but King George hoped to demonstrate his respect for the other branch of the armed forces by enrolling William in the Navy. The foundations of a reputable career would thus be laid for his son, for the King was well aware that Parliament was in no mood to grant sufficient funds for all his children to subsist parasitically on the public purse. Besides, King George was anxious that his male offspring should offer a worthy example to his subjects by their diligent pursuit of suitable employment; his sons should be a credit to the nation, not a burden on it. There was, in addition, another motive

Alphabetical counters used by the children of George III. Both King George and Queen Charlotte took an active interest in the education of their children, and William's scholastic progress was carefully monitored by his parents.

The Old Palace, Kew, home of King George III and Queen Charlotte. In 1772 William and his younger brother Edward moved from here to their own establishment on nearby Kew Green, but every morning they breakfasted with their parents at the Palace.

behind his decision to send William to sea. The Prince of Wales already showed signs of maturing into a sophisticated reprobate: by early 1779 he was accredited with the seduction of at least one maid of honour. The King had directed a blistering epistle to his heir, complaining of his inattention to his studies, his casual attitude towards his religious devotions and, above all, his 'love of dissipation', but he feared it would have little effect. He was determined, however, to prevent his amiable but impressionable third son from being ensnared by the glistening web of vice and self-indulgence spun by the decadent eldest brother. A career at sea would effectively remove William from the sphere of temptation.

Accordingly, on 15 June 1779, William was conducted to Spithead by General Budé and there received on Admiral Robert Digby's ship, named, inappropriately enough, the *Prince George*. Having led such a sheltered existence, the Prince might well have regarded a meeting with new shipmates as something of an ordeal, but lack of self-confidence was never

22

one of his traits. 'I went away to every part of the ship where I was received with universal joy', he noted with complacency in his first log-book. Certainly he was careful to avoid alienating his new colleagues by standing on formality: on being asked how they should address him, he bravely replied, 'I am entered as Prince William Henry but my father's name is Guelph and therefore if you please you may call me William Guelph for I am nothing more than a sailor like yourselves.'

William was only thirteen when he joined the crew of the *Prince George* as a midshipman, but such an early introduction to a seafaring life was by no means unusual. In naval circles it was widely felt to be desirable that a new recruit should gain some maritime experience before he was fourteen, and most ships carried a schoolmaster to ensure that the education of the young midshipmen was not neglected. The junior midshipmen were usually enrolled in the service by their parents, and were drawn

The royal family. A collection of portraits painted by Gainsborough in the autumn of 1782 showing the King and Queen and thirteen of their fifteen children.

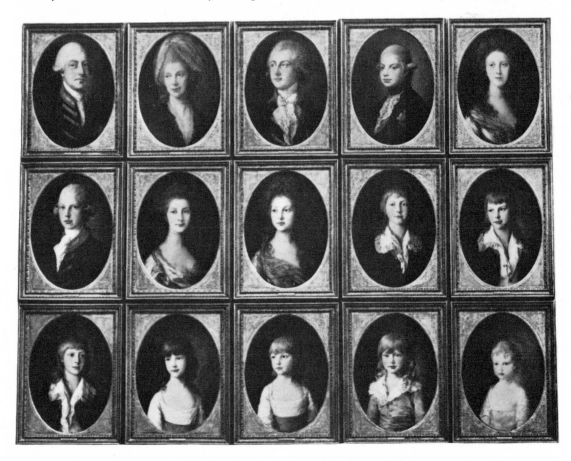

largely from the nobility, the landed gentry or the professional classes. They were billeted on board in the midshipmen's mess, a cramped dingy den, generally below the water level, suffused with a pestilential stench from the bilges and the stink of rancid butter and cheese stored in the nearby purser's store-room. The midshipmen were served with the same rations as were issued to the men: ship's biscuits alive with weevils; meat as hard as mahogany and popularly believed to be salt horse; and almost inedible oatmeal gruel. Fortunately for William, his status insured that he was frequently invited to dine at the Admiral's table, where somewhat choicer fare was served; and a special cabin was set aside in which he could pursue his studies with the faithful Mr Henry Majendie, who had dutifully accompanied his royal pupil when he embarked upon his naval career.

William soon settled in his new life, enjoying fishing overboard and indulging in rather elementary horseplay. He soon found out, however, that there was more to naval service than cutting down his slumbering shipmates' hammocks and brawling in the mess: the colonists' rebellion in America had matured into a full scale war against Britain in which the Navy was acutely involved. The British defeat at Saratoga in 1777 had indicated that the English could expect a long-drawn-out struggle with the rebels, and the French had determined to cash in on British difficulties and ally themselves with the Americans. By 1779 both the French and their allies, the Spaniards, were embroiled in the struggle against the British, who now reverted to a policy of keeping a few footholds on the American coast and pursuing primarily a naval war. The British Navy was therefore confronted with the necessity of performing a multiplicity of tasks: keeping ships continuously at sea to supply the garrisons in America; fighting the French in the West Indies; supplying Gibraltar, currently besieged by the Spaniards; guarding the Channel and endeavouring to keep the French fleet bottled up in its home ports. Even in peacetime, sailors were at the mercy of the elements – William himself nearly drowned when the *Prince George* narrowly escaped collision with another ship in the fleet in a storm off Cape Finisterre – but when William went to sea the additional exorbitant demands imposed upon the fleet by the war ensured that naval service was fraught with both challenge and danger.

opposite A contemporary engraving depicting Prince William Henry being instructed by Admiral Digby on board the *Prince George*.

William's first experience as an active seaman was somewhat dispiriting. The *Prince George* sailed to join the Channel fleet, whose instructions were to prevent the meeting of the French and Spanish fleets during the summer. It failed in this endeavour, and the British fleet was obliged to withdraw to Plymouth before the combined might of the enemy. An invasion scare ensued as the new armada approached English shores, but fortunately sickness in their ranks prevented the foreign fleets from pressing their advantage, and they returned to their home ports. The crisis over, William was granted leave, spending the Christmas of 1779 with his parents.

After this brief rest he returned to duty, and his ship now joined the fleet setting out under the command of Rodney to relieve Gibraltar. This second cruise was more successful. On the passage out the fleet fell in with a Spanish convoy protected by seven men-of-war, and the British succeded in capturing a total of twenty-two enemy ships. Rodney informed the King that one of the men-of-war had been re-christened the *Prince William*, 'in whose presence she had the honour to be taken'. Even more excitement lay in store. The fleet continued to sail along the coast of Portugal, and on 16 January 1789 the Spanish fleet was sighted off Cape St Vincent. Rodney pursued them and successfully engaged. William was exhilarated by his first taste of battle: 'Won't we give these haughty dons a thrashing!' he called to a nearby officer as the encounter began. The *Prince George*'s role in the engagement was, in fact, comparatively minor; nevertheless, one member of the crew was killed and three others suffered mutilation. William was by no means inured to the horrors of war. He wrote to his father that he had witnessed the explosion that had destroyed the Spanish ship *Santo Domingo*, 'a most shocking and dreadful sight'. But his youthful sensitivity should not be exaggerated: on the whole his attitude to the battle seems to have been that of any schoolboy at a college rugger match. Admiral Digby noted robustly, 'The moment he saw that they were preparing for action his spirits rose to that degree that he was almost in a state of insanity . . . the moment the fleets were separated, his spirits sunk very low.'

The fleet duly proceeded to Gibraltar, relieving the besieged garrison on the island before setting back for England in February. By May 1780 William was safely home again. He was summoned to London, where he ceremoniously presented his father with the captured flag of the Spanish Admiral. He found that accounts of his involvement at the battle had made him something of a hero: when he attended a performance of *The Tempest* in Drury Lane he was greeted with such tumultuous enthusiasm that several members of the audience only narrowly escaped asphyxiation. Such agreeable interludes were, however, rare, for the call of duty ensured that the Prince spent more time afloat than accepting the plaudits of the masses in London. From May until August 1780 he cruised desultorily in the Channel, and then joined the fleet engaged in protecting the homeward-bound West Indian fleet. In December he was granted leave to spend Christmas with his parents.

It was during these holidays that William became involved in what turned out to be the first of many amorous encounters. In January 1781 William was observed animatedly dancing with Miss Julia Fortescue at a ball given at St James's Palace in honour of the Queen's birthday. His parents were quick to take alarm at this innocent adolescent infatuation, particularly when it was rumoured that William wished to marry the young lady. The Prince must be swiftly despatched to sea, they decreed, before he could entangle himself further. By the end of the month William was back on board the *Prince George*, which cruised in the Channel for six weeks before joining the fleet under Admiral Darby, sailing south and participating once again in the relief of Gibraltar. By early summer the Prince's ship had returned to Spithead, although his duties prevented him from hastening to London. In King George's opinion, however, his son was too close for comfort. Service on waters close to home afforded William too much opportunity for dalliance with nubile young ladies during his leave, while it did not guarantee his freedom from the pernicious influence of the Prince of Wales. A remoter posting must be found. Accordingly, when Admiral Digby was given command of an American station, King George determined that William should accompany him across the Atlantic. On 24 August 1781, the Prince, aged just sixteen, arrived in Sandy Hook, New York.

At that time New York was in loyalist hands, but New Jersey, just across the Hudson River, was controlled by the rebels. William's presence would, it was hoped, give a boost to

English troops landing in New York during the American War of Independence. In the summer of 1781 New York was still held by supporters of the crown, and King George III decided to send William to visit the port to encourage the loyalists in their struggle against the rebels.

the morale of the beleaguered crown supporters. The wisdom of the move at first seemed undeniable, for the citizens received the royal representative with touchingly enthusiastic demonstrations, while loyal preachers poured fulsome eulogies on his head from the pulpit. William spent the autumn and early winter of 1782 studying in Admiral Digby's house, diverting himself with aimless wanders around the town or an occasional visit to a nearby frozen lake, where agile attendants propelled him across the ice on a special chair equipped with runners. William's presence in America had not, however, eluded the rebels, and his visit to New York nearly culminated in serious embarrassment for King George and his cause in the war. Colonel Ogden, a daring rebel officer, conceived the plan of stealing over from New Jersey in whale-boats and seizing Prince William and Admiral Digby as they lay in their quarters in town. Washington himself warmly endorsed this audacious proposal, although he stipulated that no harm must come to either of the prisoners. What he intended to do with his captives remains obscure, as fortunately the British authorities learnt of the plot and foiled the conspirators by placing an extra guard on the Admiral's house.

Even this excitement could not prevent the Prince from finding the small settlement at New York dull. He therefore requested to be transferred to service on board the fifty-gun *Warwick* commanded by Captain Elphinstone, later created Lord Keith. Elphinstone was known to be a stern disciplinarian, but William nevertheless succeeded in gaining his approval on the ensuing cruise off the coast of Virginia, a highlight of which was the capture of a French frigate, *L'Aigle*. The Prince of Wales communicated to his brother Frederick that he had received intelligence from Elphinstone that enabled him to conclude that there could not be 'a more gallant or a better officer than our dear William is already and promises to be'. In fact, when William came into contact with those that he had the sense to realize had truly superior minds, such as Elphinstone or Nelson, he usually gained from the association. Unfortunately, he was too inclined to dismiss or ignore the advice of those who, although worthy men, were not necessarily of such an exceptional calibre. George III was hardly likely to welcome such discriminatory notions from his wilful son. Elphinstone remained a friend and adviser, ultimately becoming William's Treasurer and Comptroller of the Household when the Prince was created a duke.

William's service on the *Warwick* was not of long duration. On the return of Keith's squadron to Sandy Hook he was transferred, on the King's express orders, to the *Barfleur* under the command of Lord Hood, a particular favourite of King George. To the King's regret, the long-suffering Mr Majendie announced that his health did not permit him to effect the transition himself. It is unlikely that the Prince shared his father's sorrow at the tutor's departure. Doubtless he hoped it marked the beginning of an era of freedom from irksome supervision. He was swiftly disappointed. His father sternly enjoined Hood to keep a 'strict eye' on Prince William in order that he might act 'with civility and attention to all persons and avoid that familiarity which frequently borders on contempt'. Despite these precautions, the King felt that William's behaviour required extra surveillance. To the chagrin of both Lord Hood and William himself, King George selected a certain Captain Napier to monitor the Prince's conduct on board the *Barfleur*.

On 23 November 1782 the *Barfleur* sailed for Jamaica. The trip began with a disappointment for William, for news came through that peace had been concluded with all combatants in the American war, and any hopes the Prince might have enjoyed of gaining glory in a warlike encounter now seemed doomed to failure. But personal problems also loomed large for him on the trip. Almost inevitably, the tension between Lord Hood and Prince William on the one hand and Captain Napier on the other erupted into open disagreement. William wrote hotly to his father, indignantly outlining Captain Napier's failings. Hood supported the Prince, assuring the King of Napier's intolerance and lack of tact, and he was delighted when Napier finally requested to leave the ship. King George, however, did not regard the incident as closed. In April 1783 he wrote severely of William to Hood, 'I cannot admire the warmth he has shown in his disputes with Captain Napier, of which his own account to me bears the strongest marks.' He added grimly, 'William has ever been violent when controlled', and the incident served to convince the King that something more extreme than the discipline of a man-of-war would be necessary to improve his impetuous son's character.

Nevertheless, the West Indian cruise was not uniformly unfortunate. In November 1782 Captain Nelson had arrived at Sandy Hook, and his ship accompanied the *Barfleur* to the Caribbean. Nelson made an instant impression on the Prince, partly on account of his quaintly outmoded style of dress and youthful appearance ('He appeared to be the merest boy of a captain I ever beheld', William later recalled), but also through the exertion of his powerful charm. Years after, William was to reminisce, 'there was something irresistibly pleasing in his address and conversation; and an enthusiasm, when speaking on professional subjects that showed he was no common being.' Nelson too, was much taken by the royal midshipman, writing to a friend, 'He will be, I am certain, an ornament to our service. He is a seaman, which you could hardly suppose, with every other qualification you may expect of him; but he will be a disciplinarian, and a strong one. . . . With the best temper, and great good sense, he cannot fail of being pleasing to everyone.' It was a prophecy that was to prove sadly inaccurate.

The inhabitants of Jamaica went out of their way to be agreeable. The House of Assembly read him a graceful speech of welcome, and the prosperous planters eagerly entertained their visitor at a series of levées. He also visited Dominica and, at the invitation of its Spanish Governor, Havannah. The freshly established cordial relations between Britain and Spain were

Horatio Nelson by J. F. Rigaud. The young Captain Nelson first met William in November 1782 and accompanied him on his subsequent Caribbean cruise. Even on this first meeting, Nelson was favourably impressed by the royal midshipman, and William himself was struck by Nelson's charm.

nearly endangered when William was observed to be paying marked attention to Maria, enchanting daughter of the Spanish Admiral Solano, but Nelson had the Prince whisked off the island before he could offend any Spanish notions of etiquette.

In the meantime, King George had been meditating on the future of his son. He had decided that William's education must be concluded abroad, but away from the rowdiness and profanity that characterized the midshipmen's mess. The King hoped that a continental tour and a prolonged spell in Hanover would endow William with that patina of refinement that the quarterdeck of a man-of-war had so markedly failed to provide. William accompanied his division home at the end of the West Indian cruise, docking at Spithead in June 1783, and set off to pay a farewell visit to his family prior to his departure for the Continent. His parents afforded him a cool reception: on arriving at St James's Palace after an absence of two years, Prince William was greeted with a message that his parents would receive him at a specified hour. When eventually the meeting took place King George was severely critical of his son's lack of certain social graces, his bad language and his uncouth manners. The reunion with his brothers and sisters was more agreeable, if all too brief. In July 1783 Prince William embarked for Hanover, the chrysalis from which his father fondly hoped he would emerge 'the Prince, the gentleman and the officer'.

31

2 The Prince, the Gentleman and the Officer

WILLIAM WAS ACCOMPANIED to Hanover by General Budé and Captain William Merrick, a cheerful officer whose company was infinitely more congenial to the Prince than that of his former instructor. King George outlined to Budé an ambitious curriculum for William to pursue while abroad, explaining that he hoped that his son would emerge from Hanover with a thorough mastery of 'the German language, the law of nations, the grounds of civil law, engineering, artillery and military tactics'. A visit to some of the foreign courts in Europe was also on the schedule, and the King hoped that during his Grand Tour William would absorb some of the elegance and refinement of those establishments.

The King was reassured by the fact that, in addition to the supervision of his official travelling companions, William's initiation into the princely graces would be monitored by his elder brother Frederick, who was already living in Hanover and whose deportment most closely approximated to King George's idea of a dutiful, loyal and affectionate son. The lay Bishop of Osnaburgh fully shared his father's belief that William lacked sophistication: in August 1783 he wrote testily to the Prince of Wales that William was 'so excessively rough and rude that there was no bearing it'. But it soon became apparent that mere brotherly disapproval and a spell abroad could not affect the metamorphosis in William's demeanour that his father so earnestly desired. William himself was by no means consistent in his efforts at self-amelioration, and the habits of the quarterdeck were deeply ingrained. Frederick steadily relayed to his father a series of discouraging and disloyal letters on William's progress; certainly the two years that William spent abroad were singularly unsuccessful in instilling in him the suave bearing of the accomplished courtier.

The reasons for this failure were various. The King's selection of travelling companions was unfortunate: William resented his renewed thraldom to General Budé, whom he regarded as an unwelcome relic from his childhood. Budé still tried to exercise a considerable measure of control over his pupil, but William preferred to ignore the restrictions imposed by the stern old gentleman and instead refer for advice to the 'faithful Merrick', infinitely more complaisant in his attitude to William's escapades and occasionally featuring as an accomplice in them.

preceding pages Prince William Henry in naval uniform.

34

Gambling in the late eighteenth century. Prince William became involved in gaming circles while in Hanover, but he soon incurred heavy losses at the hands of more experienced players. To King George's chagrin, General Budé was obliged to intervene to extricate William from his debts.

When the General attempted to forbid William from going out alone, the Prince wrote to his eldest brother with ominous arrogance, 'I soon cut him short and have done exactly as I like best'. With the Prince in this frame of mind it was hardly likely that he would meekly submit to the rigorous programme of improvement devised by his father.

The truth was that William regarded his period abroad as an opportunity to enjoy all the pleasures afforded by a life on shore, to which he had hitherto been denied access. Unfortunately his father had granted him only a meagre allowance of £100 a year, and this sum was quite insufficient to cope with the expenses entailed in the pursuit of these exciting new occupations. He acquired from Frederick a taste for gambling, but his luck was bad, and soon General Budé was forced to apply for royal permission to liquidate the debts accumulated at the table. Predictably this resulted in a searing admonition from King George: 'I cannot too strongly set before your eyes that if you continue to indulge every foolish idea you must be wretched all your life . . .' thundered his enraged parent. 'In you I fear that vanity which has been too predominant in your character has

occasioned this, but I hope in the future you will be wiser.'
Penitently William promised to be more prudent, but to King
George the incident seemed depressingly familiar, a painful
reminder of the path of extravagant degeneration followed by
his eldest son.

Unfortunately William found singularly unappealing those
occupations he could with propriety pursue. He was no
horseman, and the daily inspection of the famous cream-
coloured horses of the royal stables did not enthral him. He
disliked hunting, and shooting was abandoned when he
complained that the recoil of the gun hurt his shoulder. Nor did
his studies absorb him, for he found Vauban on fortification a
dull business. He grumbled to his brother George of the
stultifying boredom of Hanoverian life: 'Pretty qualifications to
be sure for any young man like me, smoaking, playing at
twopenny whist, and wearing great thick boots! Oh! I wish I
was returned: England, England for ever and the pretty girls of
Westminster!'

Nor did that intercourse with the German aristocracy, which
the King so fervently hoped would improve his son, compensate, in Prince William's opinion, for his absence from
home. He had tried to make a success of his relationships in
Germany, and at first had made an effort to overcome the
xenophobia that was already a feature of his character. In
January 1784 he wrote to his brother with studied fairness, 'An
honest man, whether an Englishman or a German, is still an
honest man, and there are a great many such here; therefore it is
my own fault if I keep company with bad ones.' Alas, this
becoming fit of resolution did not endure. In January 1785 he
confided to the Prince of Wales that he found the German
nobility pompous, haughty and proud; they in their turn
objected to William's unmannered turn of phrase. 'My free
tongue with the English oaths did not go down with the *Vons*,'
he admitted, 'so I left them short there and associated myself
with the second class.' Unfortunately 'blasted spies' ensured that
the King heard of William's cheerful renunciation of aristocratic German society, and in consequence he penned 'a most
serious and alarming letter' to his erring son, rebuking him for
his taste for low company and even threatening to promote one
of his younger brothers to a rank in the Navy senior to his own.

36

'What an event!' wrote William in mortification and alarm to his sympathetic eldest brother.

The Prince, in fact, had cultivated acquaintances of a sort that would have alarmed his father still more had he been fully aware of their details. In April 1784 William wrote significantly to the Prince of Wales, 'I have introduced myself into the private parties of the women'. There is no doubt that any sexual experience that William had managed to pick up in brothels while on service in foreign ports was greatly furthered by his association with the *demi-monde* in Hanover. But although he might have gratified his ample sexual energies with casual amours of this nature, the Prince's attentions to his studies were diverted by other, more consequential, encounters. Fairly soon after his arrival he was enchanted by his cousin Charlotte, daughter of Prince Charles of Mecklenburg-Strelitz. Marriage, however, formed no part of his parents' plans for his immediate future, and Queen Charlotte was firmly dismissive when she heard of the matter. 'You are of an age when young men are apt to fancy themselves in love with every sprightly young woman they see', she wrote, warning him to forbear from pressing his suit. Her diagnosis seemed correct when, in the winter of 1784, the ardent Prince was regularly to be seen escorting Maria Schindbach as she sped in her sledge along the frozen streets, a romance that was shattered by her engagement to Captain Merrick.

The facts surrounding another of the Prince's alleged entanglements remain shrouded in mystery. Caroline von Linsingen, daughter of Lieutenant-General Wilhelm von Linsingen, Commander of the Twelfth Hanoverian Infantry and an intimate of the ducal family of Mecklenburg-Strelitz, recorded in a series of exaggeratedly sentimental letters that William had secretly married her at a dawn service in a chapel near Pyrmont. According to her, the Prince had obligingly refrained from consummating the marriage for nearly a year, but after that she swiftly conceived, only to miscarry in the autumn. The couple were then separated and William allegedly returned to England heartbroken, to brood in misery on this enforced estrangement. The veracity of this moving tale is undermined by the fact that in August 1791, the time when Caroline recollects William tremulously pronouncing his vows in the mountain chapel, he was already laying siege to Mrs Jordan. Throughout her account, William behaves in a manner comparable to the hero of a Gothic romance, a style far removed from his usual rather bumbling gallantry. He remained friends with the Linsingen family in later years, and although he might have enjoyed a flirtation with their daughter on his German visit it seems certain that the incident was later greatly magnified by Caroline's fertile imagination.

The consequences, however, of another of the Prince's amatory exploits abroad are indisputable. He was obliged to accept paternity of a boy brought over from Germany a few years later by his unknown mother. He appears to have been brought up in William's household and was subsequently enlisted in the Navy. He served in the *Blenheim* and was drowned off Madagascar in 1808.

With all these distractions it is hardly surprising that William did not emerge the accomplished Prince of his father's visions. His periods in Hanover had been interspersed with a visit to Berlin, attendance at the Imperial Review in Prague and an improving tour of Switzerland, Piedmont and Savoy. In the Prince's eyes none of these excursions justified his exile abroad, and he found the intervening time spent in Hanover increasingly irksome. As early as July 1784 he was so fed up with the 'phlegmatick ways of the Germans' that he wrote fruitlessly to Lord Hood, pleading with him to secure his recall. By April 1785 he was desperate. But his father remained obdurate that William should stay abroad, and it was in fact only the disloyal intervention of Frederick that shook his determination. Frederick, by now Duke of York, urged his father to summon William home to resume his naval career, insisting that only the discipline of service on the high seas could prevent William from gratifying 'his natural inclination for all kinds of dissipation'. Reluctantly, the King agreed that William should depart for England on 20 May, and there submit to an examination by the full board of the Admiralty to secure his promotion to the rank of Lieutenant. He made it clear, however, that his son returned in disgrace: he sternly insisted that William must remain at either Kew or Windsor during the entirety of his stay in England to ensure the propriety of his conduct.

This stipulation was rigidly enforced. On William's first

Sir Joshua Reynolds'
portrait of Frederick,
William's elder brother
and companion in
Hanover. Lay Bishop of
Osnaburgh and
subsequently created Duke
of York, Frederick was
King George's favourite
son, and shared his father's
low opinion of William's
rough manners.

night home the Prince of Wales was due to host a sumptuous fête at Carlton House, and an invitation was issued to his younger brother. 'Eh, what!' expostulated the King, 'Take William away! He shan't go – he shan't go! Just arrived from Hanover – want to know how things are going on there. Fine stud! Fine stud! . . . better with his mother tonight.' Prince William could hardly be expected to agree, but his time in England was perforce spent very quietly. On 17 June 1785 he satisfied the examining board and was promoted to the rank of Lieutenant. After a 'very grand public breakfast' given in celebration by the Prince of Wales, he was hustled off to Portsmouth to join the crew of the *Hebe*, a forty-four-gun frigate.

The *Hebe* now set out from Portsmouth to accomplish a circumnavigation of England and Scotland. The trip afforded William a glimpse of life in the remoter areas of what would ultimately be his kingdom, an insight by no means common to previous British sovereigns. It was not an entirely agreeable revelation: he was shocked by the poverty of the inhabitants of the Orkneys, and surprised that His Majesty's subjects who watched him wade ashore to shoot wildfowl on the Scottish Fair Isle had no notion who he was. The cruise had less harrowing moments – he enjoyed fishing at Lewes and a ball at Haverfordwest – and by September 1785 he was safely back at Spithead.

The Prince spent the autumn of 1785 stationed at Portsmouth, going on shore whenever his duties would permit, and expressed his contentment at this situation to his eldest brother. His time on shore was spent mainly at the house of Mr Henry Martin, resident Commissioner to the Navy at Portsmouth, a family man with two daughters of about Prince William's age. In November William was enthusiastically assuring the indulgent Prince of Wales that 'We dance and amuse ourselves vastly well'; but by the new year these innocent frolics had matured into something more meaningful – William's affection for Sarah Martin had markedly deepened. His intentions were entirely respectable for he later urged his brother George: 'Do not imagine I debauched the girl: such a thought did not once enter my head.' Indeed, he hoped for the association to conclude in nothing less than marriage, but Commissioner Martin was well aware that such a match would never be permitted. William rushed to Windsor in a frantic attempt to enlist parental blessing for his proposed union, but on hearing the 'very pleasant and unexpected' news of his son's latest attachment the King merely removed him to Plymouth.

The Prince passed the early months of 1786 in deep depression. He feared he could not hope for further promotion, dreaded being posted again to America, and casual promiscuity with the Plymouth whores could not erase the memory of his beloved Sarah. He considered resignation from the service, but his financial position would not admit of such a step. 'I am really unhappy; everything goes against me', he lamented to the Prince of Wales in February 1786. 'I have been obliged to leave the girl I adore; my father will not allow me to live with the brother I am in intimate friendship with, and he does not even shew me common justice . . . To be banished to America is not what I wish . . . During the bloom of youth I am not allowed to enjoy myself like any other person of my age.'

Fortunately things soon looked up. In March he was appointed to the frigate *Pegasus*, and in April 1786 he was promoted to be its Captain. Service in America seemed more palatable under such conditions and William started his command full of good intentions, expressing the pious hope to his eldest brother that he would be steadier on his return, and proudly assuring his thrifty father that his cabin was 'one of the plainest in the service'.

Accordingly the Prince departed for the 'inhospitable shores, foggy atmosphere and rugged barren cliffs of Newfoundland', where he spent the summer of 1786. These gloomy surroundings proved no impediment to the riotous celebrations of his twenty-first birthday, which occurred while he was stationed there. Officers and men became as gloriously drunk as the Prince himself, and he was hoisted on to the shoulders of the sailors to be paraded violently from one end of the ship to the other. On leaving Newfoundland he paid a fleeting visit to Halifax, Nova Scotia, and in the autumn of 1786 was ordered to the West Indies.

It was here that William renewed his relationship with Captain Nelson, then in command of the Leeward Islands station. In the ensuing six months this developed into a warm

A letter from Nelson to a friend, giving a favourable view of William's abilities and predicting a successful naval career for him. In 1786 his friendship with the Prince was enhanced when they met again in the Caribbean and sailed round the West Indian islands.

friendship based on mutual esteem. At Nelson's wedding in March 1787 William even gallantly insisted on giving away the bride. William later reminisced that it was during this period 'that I particularly observed the greatness of Nelson's superior mind. The manner in which he enforced the Navigation Act first drew my attention to the commercial interests of my country.' The two young officers sailed round the islands together and dined at each other's quarters on alternate nights, re-enacting in their conversation the details of former naval battles. Nelson fully reciprocated the Prince's regard and wrote home in warm praise of his fellow officer. 'He has his foibles, as well as private men,' he admitted, 'but they are far overbalanced by his virtues. In his professional line he is superior to two thirds, I am sure, of the list.' Nelson noted that the Prince was a stern disciplinarian, but insisted that the *Pegasus* was 'one of the finest ordered frigates I have seen'. No doubt Nelson's profound reverence for royalty, and his belief that the Prince's support would be valuable in securing future promotion, encouraged his friendship with his young companion, but his favourable assessment of William's seamanlike capabilities cannot be dismissed. Nelson was quite emphatic that William was 'steady in command and not violent', and such testimony must be considered in any evaluation of Prince William's naval career.

During his visits to the West Indian islands William plunged into a round of amusements that quite enervated the frail Nelson, who was obliged to accompany the energetic young Captain as he participated in colonial hospitality. In December 1786 Nelson wrote frankly to Fanny Nisbet, still his fiancée at the time, that only William's departure from the capital of Antigua had protected the ladies of St Johns from total collapse, so strenuous had been their exertions in the ballroom during the Prince's visit. Even William's rude health could not endure for ever the strain of attending to his duties and participating in such a full social life. By the summer of 1787 he was troubled by a severe attack of prickly heat, 'so that I had large blotches almost as big as a shilling . . . attended by such violent heat and itching as to prevent most effectually my sleeping'. His condition worsened; he lost his appetite and developed large boils, a high fever and rheumatic pains. These distressing symptoms were at least partially self-inflicted: the Prince's frequent visits to West Indian brothels had temporarily resulted in a venereal infection.

He was also troubled with financial worries. In 1786 his father and Pitt had granted him an allowance of £3,500 per annum, but this proved quite insufficient to prevent him from tumbling into debt. He lamented tragically to the Prince of Wales that if his position did not improve he would have to resign the command of his ship and plant cabbages for his subsistence.

Another problem intruded to mar the Prince's enjoyment of the Caribbean. His relations with the men under his command

Like William, the Prince of Wales was frequently in debt, and in the summer of 1786 he was forced to leave London for Brighton in order to cut back his expenses. The satirists treated his retirement with some derision, but William was impressed by his brother's attempt at economy. 'I commend you extreamly,' he wrote loyally from abroad, 'as do the British nation.'

had sharply deteriorated. William once wrote to his sister Mary 'I doat to see my men happy', and there is no doubt that in some respects William was a thoroughly conscientious officer. Sir Thomas Byam Martin, who served under the Prince as a midshipman, concedes that William took great pains to ensure that the youngsters on his ship were well instructed in seamanship and that their education was not neglected. On the other hand, it is clear that William's volatile and sudden temperament did not entirely fit him for the pressures of high rank. Against Nelson's favourable assessment of William one must weigh the verdict of Byam Martin, who was to have a distinguished career, and who asserted that William 'was deficient in almost all the qualities necessary for a person in high command'. William was always a firm Captain, but it appears that his rule became unreasonably imperious after the arrival of the *Pegasus* in the Leeward Islands. It is probable that William wished to impress his friend Nelson with the good order of his ship, and in so doing lost a sense of proportion in matters of discipline. All his Lieutenants were resentful that his delight in

44

Nelson's company kept them from his table, but his First Lieutenant, Isaac Schomberg, was particularly affronted by William's management of his ship. Schomberg, an experienced but overbearing officer some years William's senior, conceived it his duty to guide his Captain during his first term of command, but William naturally resented his advice. The Prince recounted that on one occasion Schomberg intervened when William intended to discipline a seaman, saying 'If WE punished for every trifling offence WE should make ourselves unpopular and be constantly punishing'. The Lieutenant was probably right, but he expressed himself tactlessly. By the time the *Pegasus* reached the West Indies there was already considerable hostility between William and Schomberg; Nelson noticed the almost palpable tension on board when he met William in Dominica in December 1786. In early January Schomberg narrowly escaped court-martial, but within a week he decided that his position under William was so intolerable that he would appeal over his Captain's head for just such a trial. Nelson was annoyed at what he regarded as Schomberg's frivolous appeal for justice in such a remote station, and he ordered the Lieutenant's close confinement. Thus imprisoned, Schomberg repented of his hasty step, but by now William was not prepared to let the matter drop. With Nelson's agreement he sailed for Jamaica in an attempt to have Schomberg tried, but fortunately the tactful Commodore Gardner there induced him to accept a suitable apology from his First Lieutenant. The Admiralty, however, had not been impressed by William's tenacity, obviously suspecting that Schomberg had some grounds for complaint. Lord Hood signified his disapproval by subsequently appointing Schomberg his Lieutenant on the *Barfleur*, and William hardly made amends by despatching him a resentful letter threatening to resign if he did not receive a 'satisfactory explanation' for this appointment. Even the unfortunate Nelson, rebuked for permitting the Prince's departure to the Jamaican station, urged him to forgive Schomberg, but William remained obdurate: 'I am by no means of a revengeful temper', he asserted with assurance, 'what I did, I did for the good of His Majesty's service and most certainly shall do again'. In fairness to William, Schomberg clearly was a difficult officer with whom to share his first

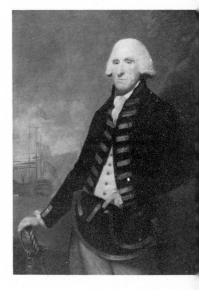

A painting by Lemuel Francis Abbott of Viscount Hood, a staunch supporter of William when he served under him as a midshipman on the *Barfleur*, but one who nevertheless disapproved of William's disciplinary action against his First Lieutenant, Schomberg.

command – his arrogant impertinence resulted later in Cornwallis sending him home in disgrace from India – but the Prince's resolute refusal to compromise over the issue did little to further his career.

Having spent a fortnight in Jamaica William sailed north, duly arriving in Halifax, Nova Scotia. He had already briefly called there and had pronounced it 'a very gay and lively place full of women, and those of the most obliging kind'. He had no cause to revise his verdict during this visit. There he made the acquaintance of Lieutenant William Dyott, who, somewhat overawed by the companionship of 'so great a person', admiringly chronicled the Prince's progress of drink and debauchery throughout his summer on the American station. Dyott insists that at this stage William himself was a moderate drinker, rarely venturing beyond a bottle of Madeira, but he delighted to see all about him quite incapacitated with liquor. At all-male dinners on his boat William would remorselessly propose repeated toasts, with the result, on one occasion at least,

Slaves working on a cotton plantation. During his visits to the West Indies, William inspected several plantations and became a convinced supporter of slavery. An opponent of slavery later tartly remarked on his attitude: 'Being a careless superficial observer, he came home under the impression that the slaves were the happiest people in the world.'

that some of his guests had to be hoisted on their chairs before pledging a final bumper.

However the Prince did not confine himself to these masculine pleasures. He delighted in attending balls and excelled at dancing – with all the pretty women in the room. Furthermore, as Dyott archly records, 'He would go into any house where he saw a pretty girl, and was perfectly acquainted with every house of a certain description in the town.' Nor was this all. After he had been ten days in Halifax he made the acquaintance of Mrs Wentworth. The racy wife of the Surveyor-General on the station, she had the reputation of being 'fonder of our sex than her own', and proved to be most amenable to the advances of the fair-haired young Prince. Her husband fortunately seemed blind to her inconstancies, but William paraded his intimacy with this sophisticated older woman with such indiscretion that surely even he must have suspected that something was amiss.

In August this happy period was terminated when the Prince was posted to Quebec. There the colonists zealously staged a re-enactment of Wolfe's capture of the city; four hundred Indian braves were assembled, that they might observe 'one in whose veins flowed the same blood as in the body of their Great Father in the East, meaning your Majesty'.

That autumn the Prince sailed for Jamaica. Then, in early November, he abruptly departed on a course for home. It was rumoured at the time, and has been accepted by most of the Prince's biographers, that this action was dictated by a selfish whim; that the young Captain, sick of his exile abroad, sailed on impulse for the delights of London. William's latest biographer, Philip Ziegler, was the first to question the justice of these aspersions, and indeed an examination of the correspondence of George III amply proves they have no foundation. In the autumn of 1787 it seemed that war was imminent between Britain and Holland on account of some misunderstanding about the navigation of the Scheldt. In early November William was secretly ordered to proceed to Ireland so that he might take part in any action that ensued. He did not particularly welcome this recall, especially as by the time the *Pegasus* had crossed the Atlantic the disagreement with Holland had been settled. In early December he wrote to his father from

Cork harbour, 'On the 11th November I received secret orders from Commodore Sawyer to proceed without loss of time to Cork or Kinsale, and there remain till further orders. I am always ready to serve wherever Your Majesty thinks proper for me to be employed, but if I was permitted to express a wish, the service abroad is far more desirable than at home, because officers pay closer and greater attention in the one than in the other.'

This zeal for service overseas was partly motivated by the Prince's alarm at the thought of a confrontation with his father, whose ears had been regularly outraged by reports of his son's debts and dissipation while abroad. William wrote gloomily to his eldest brother on the prospect of a visit to Windsor, 'There can be no great pleasure in going, with a certainty that my Christmas box or New Year's gift will be a family lecture for immorality, vice, dissipation and expence, and that I shall meet the appellation of the prodigal son.' Accordingly, when the *Pegasus* was ordered to proceed to Plymouth, William decided to plead that pressure of work prevented him from visiting his parents. Insisting that he must supervise the ship's refitting, he wrote to his father, 'It is by no means my intention to ask for leave of absence unless Your Majesty requires my presence at home.' It turned out that the King had no desire to renew the acquaintance of the son who had passed the last two years so lamentably. When the *Pegasus* docked at Plymouth on 27 December 1787 William remained in port.

He received, however, an affectionate welcome from the Prince of Wales and the Duke of York, who hurried to Plymouth to greet their long absent younger brother. Two joyous days were spent carousing in their company before they left the Prince to attend to his duties. William began to find service in England by no means so uncongenial as he had expected. In January 1788 he became enamoured of Miss Sally Winne, the attractive daughter of a well-to-do tradesman, and spent hours with his new beloved while his midshipmen waited impatiently outside on his barge. His duties also kept him busy, and in March 1788 the crew of the *Pegasus* were transferred to the *Andromeda*, a thirty-two-gun frigate. William was disappointed that he had not been given command of the larger and grander *Melampus*, but he found some compensation in fitting out his

opposite Rachel Pringle of Barbados, proprietress of a celebrated brothel in Bridgetown to which William and a group of rowdy companions paid a visit in 1786. They caused £700 worth of damage, and the formidable Rachel demanded that the Prince should compensate her in full.

men in exquisite uniforms, requiring them to wear such excruciatingly tight breeches that they could barely climb the rigging.

The months passed pleasantly enough in this way. The Queen wrote affectionately to her son, and William felt he could afford to mock the grumbles and rebukes at his debts and extravagance that still emanated from the 'old boy' at Windsor. 'Fatherly admonitions at our time of life are very unpleasant and of no use', he philosophized to the Prince of Wales; 'It is a pity he should expend his breath or his time in such fruitless labour. I wonder which of us two he looks upon with least eyes of affection.' However, William was over-sanguine about his freedom from parental control. News of his son's association with Miss Winne filtered to the King. 'Aye, what! What! What!' ejaculated King George; 'What, William playing the fool again! Send him off to America and forbid the return of the ship to Plymouth.' William had spent most of July cruising with Admiral Leveson Gower's squadron, but was looking forward to his imminent return to Miss Winne's arms. His hopes were dramatically dashed when a ship bearing express orders from Windsor approached, and he learned that he was to depart for America immediately without even returning to Plymouth to re-victual. This enforced separation was a bitter blow, but to his credit William thought also of his crew, writing to his father with dignity, 'With respect to myself I cannot help feeling it, but the situation of the officers and men under my command is very different from their having been naturally led to suppose some little time would have been given after our cruise to prepare themselves for a foreign voyage.'

Thus, in August 1788, William found himself once again at Halifax, greatly to the delight of Lieutenant Dyott, if to his own chagrin. The squadron there was under the command of Captain Sandys, a vulgar, drunken dolt, and under his influence William abandoned his usual moderation in drink. 'I never saw a man get so completely drunk', Dyott joyously recorded after a convivial dinner at the Chief Justice's. At a particularly drunken banquet that William attended in September the guests were so utterly inebriated that they failed to hear the booming distress signals from a ship foundering nearby. Fortunately the Prince departed for Jamaica in November,

opposite Prince William Henry by George Morland.

51

The Prince of Wales on
horseback, painted by
George Stubbs. Although
infinitely more
sophisticated than his
boisterous younger
brother, the Prince of
Wales felt great affection
for William, and when his
father fell ill he hastened to
summon him back from
service abroad.

where as usual he was hospitably welcomed by the prosperous
planters, who presented him with a star of the order of the
garter set in diamonds.

It was while he was cruising in the West Indies that he
received the news of his father's first attack of insanity. The
Prince was deeply shocked by the news, and although of late he
had not been on good terms with King George his distress was
genuine. 'Sincerely do I love this good and worthy man and
long may he yet with his usual firmness reign over us', he wrote
to the Prince of Wales in January 1789. He was also deeply
concerned at the plight of 'that dear inestimable woman, the
Queen'. Yet despite the fact that his concern for 'this valuable
man' was sincere, only his absence from home precluded his
active involvement in the squalid intrigues emanating from the

efforts of the Prince of Wales and his cronies to secure full powers for the Regent. As it was, William congratulated his brother on his firm stand and was anxious to return home to participate in the fruits of the new regime: 'I only hope to be admitted of the party', he wrote home humbly.

The Prince of Wales was delighted at the prospect of having another ally by his side, even one who lacked the subtle mental penetration of Fox or Sheridan. In February he issued orders to the Admiralty to summon his brother home. William hastened to comply, but by the time the *Andromeda* docked at Spithead on 28 April 1789 the King's recovery had quite dashed the hopes of the Prince of Wales's party. William was to spend the years ahead not basking in the warm affection of an indulgent and powerful elder brother, but in undistinguished obscurity.

Thanksgiving service at St Paul's for the recovery of George III. William had felt genuine concern for the plight of his sick father but had nonetheless looked forward to the prospect of a regency under his eldest brother, and it was noted that he played a somewhat muted role in the celebrations for his father's recovery.

53

54

3
Duke
of Clarence

THE KING'S RECOVERY of his senses entailed for William the abandonment of any rosy visions of the future conjured up by the prospect of a Regency with the Prince of Wales as head of state. A scurrilous article in *The Times* had actually asserted that William had sailed home without orders in hopes of being appointed First Lord of the Admiralty by his brother, but if it is unlikely that even he had entertained such grandiose notions, the fact that his expectations for the future again seemed decidedly bleak must have been galling indeed. His hopes now lay in securing the favour of the King, but his actions were hardly calculated to further this enterprise.

Admittedly, at first it seemed that the Prince's natural sympathy for an ailing and weakened parent would ensure his correct behaviour and endear him to the King. After one visit to his father in May 1789, the formidable keeper of the Queen's robes, Frau Schellenberg, suggested that his father's illness must have caused him deep distress. 'Yes', cried William in agreement, 'I was very sorry for His Majesty, very sorry indeed – no man loves the King better, of that you may be assured . . . And I felt for the Queen too, I did faith! I was horribly agitated when I saw the King first. I could hardly stand.'

Sadly, the temptations of ostentatiously allying himself with the Prince of Wales and the Duke of York, now in disgrace at court, quite overcame these fine sentiments. In early June the Spanish Ambassador gave a ball to celebrate the restoration of the King's health, and there it was noticed that the three eldest princes sat conspicuously apart from the rest of the royal family, declining even to dance with their sisters. The Queen still felt deeply resentful about the behaviour of her sons George and Frederick during the Regency crisis, and by behaving thus William succeeded in involving himself in the ill favour that surrounded them. Another issue aggravated his already bad relations with his parents: William felt bitter that he had not been elevated to the peerage, whereas the Duke of York had been ennobled when only twenty-one. Unwisely, he threatened to air his grievance on a public platform, taking steps to secure nomination for a parliamentary seat in Devon. Alarmed at the thought of William on a political crusade in the West Country, the King was dragooned into creating his son Duke of Clarence and St Andrews and Earl of Munster, but as he signed

preceding pages:
The Duke of Clarence by
Sir Thomas Lawrence.

56

the patent he observed with foreboding, 'I well know that is another vote added to the opposition'. And indeed, despite the fact that Parliament settled an annual income of £12,000 on the newly appointed Duke and gave him an apartment at St James's Palace and various other allowances for his table expenses, William's relations with his father did not at once improve. On 28 May he sent the King a grudging letter of thanks, incidentally announcing that his new income would be quite insufficient to keep him out of debt. The consequence was a blistering missive from his enraged parent, bitterly denouncing the conduct of his three eldest sons over the past few months. William hastily attempted to placate his father, assuring him that he had misinterpreted a letter intended to express the deepest gratitude for his undoubted munificence, but the incident poisoned their relations for some time. They were later restored to mutual feelings of grudging affection, but the King's lack of faith in William's judgement had been strongly re-inforced. Nor could the King derive any consolation from an improvement in his son's general demeanour. On his return to court William had earnestly assured Fanny Burney that he had given up his 'mad frolics', but at intervals his good nature still burst through this imposed reserve with an enthusiasm that bordered on the oafish. On one occasion the Duke of Clarence, who had been with his father, appeared, fairly drunk, in the room where Miss Burney was dining with Mrs Schellenberg and several other royal attendants, and called boisterously for champagne with which to pledge the monarch's health. The simpering equerries who were present obediently drained glass after glass, and Mrs Schellenberg felt obliged to remonstrate at such excessive conviviality. 'Hold your potato jaw, my dear!' cried the Duke jovially, and then made clumsy amends by seizing the outraged lady's hand and abruptly kissing it. Luckily he was summoned away to a ball before he could wreak more havoc.

It was perhaps fortunate that William's new status enabled him to have an establishment of his own, away from the strictures of the court. He temporarily rented Henry Hobart's house, Ivy Lodge in Richmond, before buying a house at Petersham which he renamed Clarence Lodge. He was happy with his new life in England and rejected pointed suggestions

Fanny Burney, the celebrated diarist of King George III's court, who chronicled some of William's misdemeanours.

from his father that he might find a return to active service worthwhile. He was, however, summoned from his retirement in May 1790, when he was appointed to captain the *Valiant*, following the Spanish seizure of English ships at the settlement of Nootka Sound, Vancouver Island, and the subsequent mobilization of the English fleet. The Duke did not relish the renewed demands of duty. He fretted in ports on the southern coast, waiting for the fleet to refit, and now that he had experienced the charms of Richmond the attractions of Plymouth seemed very slight. 'Not a woman fit to be touched with the tongs, not a house to put your head in after dark', he wrote crossly to his brother George; he was delighted when the threat of war receded and the *Valiant* was paid off in November. He was created a Rear Admiral in the following December, but in fact his thankful return to Clarence Lodge was to mark the end of his active naval career.

One problem, however, required solution before his contentment could be complete: the Duke required, if not a wife, at least a mate. In September 1789 he had outraged the pious Richmond matrons by installing the courtesan Polly Finch in Ivy Lodge, but the liaison had been brief. Even Miss Finch's mercenary nature could not withstand the Duke's habit of reading aloud to her from *Lives of the Admirals*, and although she endured one volume she packed her bags and fled on learning there was as much to come. Yet William still yearned for the solace of female companionship. Having had ample experience of cheap promiscuity in the course of his travels, he now looked forward to the pleasures of a more stable relationship. Marriage would seem to have been the obvious solution. Unfortunately, the Royal Marriage Act, passed in 1772 at the King's request, severely limited his choice of spouse. King George had been infuriated by the marriages of his brothers, the Dukes of Gloucester and Cumberland, to ladies whom he deemed unsuitable. The Act was therefore instituted, decreeing that in future no member of the royal family aged under twenty-five could marry without the sovereign's permission, and even after that age had been attained twelve months' notice must be given to the Privy Council, or the sanction of Parliament obtained, before a valid marriage could be contracted. The King would not countenance his sons making their

opposite Mrs Jordan playing Viola, a role that enabled her to wear breeches and show her legs to great advantage.

William's mistress, the actress Dorothy Jordan. She was particularly admired for her mastery of comic roles. In the critic Hazlitt's opinion, 'her smile had the effect of sunshine'.

selection from the daughters of the great aristocratic families of his realm; such matches might cause political tension, and besides the King preferred that royal blood should not be mingled with that flowing in more lowly veins. Marriage to a catholic would have entailed William forsaking any claim to the succession, so suitable wifely candidates were confined to the Princesses of the northern European courts. The prospect of such a match did not inspire William to insist that these establishments should be combed to provide him with a bride. The possibility of securing the celebrated actress Dorothy Jordan as his established mistress provided an alluring alternative.

In 1790 Mrs Jordan had reached the top of her career, having graced the London stage for five years. She had been born in London in 1761, one of the children resulting from an affair between Francis Bland, the disinherited son of an Irish judge, and an actress called Grace Phillips. Her father had abandoned her mother when Dorothy was thirteen, and had died four years later. Dorothy turned to her mother's old profession to support herself, and by 1779 she was on the Dublin stage. Unfortunately, Richard Daly, the lecherous manager of a stage company there, contrived to seduce her, using a mixture of flattery, threats and blackmail; in 1782, pregnant by him, she fled to England. There she joined a group of actors in the provinces and, in view of her condition, changed her name to Mrs Jordan. After three years she transferred to London to join Richard Brinsley Sheridan's company at the Theatre Royal, Drury Lane. She swiftly established herself as the foremost comic actress of the day, for although Mrs Siddons had previously dominated the London stage her genius extended mainly to tragedy, and her weeping, shuddering and swooning audiences welcomed some light relief from another talented performer. Mrs Jordan was not renowned for her beauty, but her figure and legs were unusually neat and she looked especially dashing in breeches. Furthermore her voice, and more particularly her laugh, somehow combined sensuality and gaiety. The critic Leigh Hunt insisted that her voice was 'pregnant with melody', while Hazlitt asserted that 'her smile had the effect of sunshine and her laugh did one good to hear it'. In the spring of 1790 it was remarked that the Duke of Clarence was a regular member of the audience of *The Spoil'd Child*, a production in which Mrs Jordan starred as Little Pickle. Certainly this farce was calculated to appeal to William's rather childish sense of humour: Little Pickle played a series of practical jokes, substituting his aunt's parrot for the pheasant on a spit, and removing a chair from underneath an elderly gentleman; but it was the person of Mrs Jordan rather than the merits of the script alone that ensured his repeated attendance. Enraptured by the delightful actress, William determined that she should become his constant companion.

There was, however, some delay before his courtship was successful. Initially William's recall to sea interrupted the pressing of his suit, but on his return, another, more intractable, problem remained. Soon after her 1785 London début Dorothy had set up home with Richard Ford, the inconsequential son of a physician, and by him she now had two daughters. She had always entertained hopes that the affair would conclude in marriage. Only when Ford failed to counter the ardent wooing

Sir Richard Ford, Mrs Jordan's previous lover, by whom she had two daughters. She had hoped that Ford would marry her, but his continued failure to propose persuaded her to settle for a life with William.

A VOLUPTUARY under the horrors of Digestion.

above 'A voluptuary reclining under the horrors of digestion' – a particularly malicious caricature of the Prince of Wales by Gillray. The Prince sits picking his teeth with a fork after a gargantuan meal. In the background an overflowing chamber pot acts as a paperweight for piles of unpaid bills.

left The music room at the Brighton Pavilion, designed by Nash for George IV.

La Promenade en famille, a satirical cartoon by Gillray; it shows the Duke of Clarence and Dorothy Jordan en route from Richmond to the house he acquired at Bushy in his new capacity as Ranger of Bushy Park. Mrs Jordan is reading her part as Little Pickle from the script of *The Spoil'd Child*.

of her new admirer with a concrete proposal did she abandon her hopes of wedlock and consent to move in with the Duke. On 13 October 1791, after he had been pursuing Mrs Jordan for eleven months, William wrote with satisfaction to his brother George, 'you may safely congratulate me on my success'. The new liaison did not escape the attentions of the gossip columnists. In late October *The Times* amused its readers with a report that 'A certain Duke had a private party the other evening. We can muster up the following names: Priscilla Tomboy, Miss Prue, Master Pickle, Miss Viola, Signora Hypolita, a country girl, a Virgin unmasked and Miss Hoyden – though the porter swears he only admitted ONE lady!' For the next twenty years the Duke and Mrs Jordan lived together to all intents as man and wife. In January 1794 Mrs Jordan presented William with a baby boy, named George, and in the following years he was joined by four brothers and five sisters, all named after the royal family, a brood comprising ten little Fitz-clarences in all.

One might have thought such open cohabitation would have incurred the disapproval of the King, but the monarch appears to have been gruffly understanding of his son's arrangements. He was even reputed to have enquired of William the details: 'Hey, hey! What's this – what's this? You keep an actress they say?' 'Yes, sir.' 'Ah well, well, how much do you give her, eh?' 'A thousand a year, sir.' 'A thousand, a thousand! Too much, too much! Five hundred quite enough, quite enough!' Even if it is doubtful that the King entered quite so wholeheartedly into his son's affairs he demonstrated his tolerance of the relationship when, in January 1797, he made William Ranger of Bushy Park; Lord Liverpool reported that Clarence had managed to quite reconcile his father to his lifestyle, and that the King now joked with him about Mrs Jordan. The Queen was probably more severe – as late as 1812 she appears never to have met her grandson George Fitzclarence – but even she could not resist accompanying the King on his visits to the theatre to see the famous actress; and in May 1800 all the Princesses joined their parents at Drury Lane. The occasion was somewhat marred when a lunatic attempted to murder the King, but he was overpowered and the Duke of Clarence manfully marched the captive away, leaving Mrs Jordan to conclude her performance with a rousing rendition of *God Save the King*. Predictably, William's brothers were indulgent towards his companion. A newspaper report of 1806 revealed that the Prince of Wales and the Dukes of York, Kent, Sussex and Cambridge had attended William's birthday party, and that the Prince of Wales and the Duke of York had escorted Mrs Jordan to the head of the dining table before seating themselves on either side of her and inspecting a parade of her children.

The Duke of Clarence settled to a tranquil domestic existence with his fertile concubine. It seemed that the outbreak of war with revolutionary France early in 1793 would shatter this harmonious life, for William patriotically offered his services to the fleet, and the imposing ship *London* was fitted out for his flag. But the Duke's indiscreet tongue prevented him from assuming the command. Partly motivated by his dislike of Mr Pitt, William argued to the House of Lords in June 1793 against the continuation of the war, pointing out that Holland, whose endangered state had been the original cause of England's

George III and his family at Covent Garden Theatre. In May 1800 the King and Queen and all their daughters attended a performance of a play in which Mrs Jordan starred.

hostility, was now secure. Pitt promptly informed the King that he could not tolerate a 'political Admiral', and William was denied further funds for the refitting of his ship. The Duke was greatly hurt by the rejection of his services, but it is probable that the Admiralty seized with relief the opportunity afforded by his indiscreet speech in the House to prevent his return to sea. They were worried that a King's son who had seen ten years' service would expect to be promoted to a position of real responsibility, yet they did not feel that William's naval record entitled them to entrust him with a fleet. William himself revealed his pretensions to high command when he assured Lord Moira that he was willing to serve 'could it be put on terms any way decent'; he warned that he would not be satisfied with being sent out sixth or seventh in command of the Channel fleet 'or on any mission obviously contrived for the sole purpose of keeping him out of the way', a situation in his opinion not 'becoming to a son of His Majesty who had seen a considerable share of active service'. But no suitable appointment was forthcoming, and the nearest the Duke got to active service in 1793 was escorting his sisters in a coach and six when they watched the Duke of York embark from Greenwich for his military command on the Continent. By early 1794 William was chafing at his inactivity, and in March he directed a letter to the Admiralty appealing for honourable employment, even stating that he was prepared to submit to demotion should his

66

rank prevent his obtaining the command of a ship without a squadron attached. With dignity he pleaded, 'All I require is active service, and that when my gallant countrymen are fighting the cause of their country and their sovereign, I may not have the imputation thrown upon me of living a life of inglorious ease, when I ought to be in the front of the danger', but his appeal was ignored. An approach to his father was similarly unsuccessful. In April 1794 William was made a Vice-Admiral, and in 1811 he was actually made Admiral of the Fleet, but these were empty honours, devoid of real power. Throughout the war the Duke continued to hope that advantage would be taken of his abilities, eagerly suggesting that he replace Collingwood in command of the Mediterranean and offering himself for a variety of vacant posts, but all in vain. He was forced to experience the war at second hand, eagerly perusing detailed accounts of its progress from Nelson; but the death of Nelson, at whose funeral he was observed to shed copious tears, deprived him even of this source of information.

Nelson's funeral procession. Throughout the war William had maintained a close contact with Nelson, whose letters kept him informed about its progress. Nelson had visited the Duke on his last visit to London, and his death came as a grievous blow to his friend. At Nelson's funeral the Duke was seen entering St Paul's Cathedral in tears.

On being made Ranger of Bushy Park near Hampton Court in 1797, the Duke moved Mrs Jordan and their growing family into the William and Mary mansion situated in the spacious grounds. Here, as Lord Farington noted, he lived with his mistress 'in a state of perfect domestic character', undistracted by the call of war. He found consolation for his inactivity by busily drilling a force of yeomanry raised locally and submerging himself in a new interest, farming. His relationship with Mrs Jordan matured into one of comfortable affection. As he remarked to a dinner companion, 'Mrs Jordan is a very good creature, very domestic and careful of her children. To be sure she is absurd sometimes and has her humours. But there are such things more or less in all families.' At times London abounded with rumours of jealous arguments and imminent separation, but Mrs Jordan always maintained that their life was one of perfect harmony. To her, she insisted, the Duke remained 'an example for half the fathers and husbands in the world, the best of masters, the most firm and generous of friends'. Mrs Jordan was reserved in company – indeed, some thought her boring and ill-informed – but it is probable that in the intimacy of her home she was more talkative. Indeed, she once wrote to her son George, 'Military men are as bad as ACTRESSES – they can never be quiet', presumably a teasing reference to her own garrulity. On the whole they lived withdrawn from society, the Duke retiring at eleven p.m., and Mrs Jordan jokingly suggested that they could be 'dead and buried without our friends knowing even that we had been ill'. But William was no hermit, and enjoyed being a hospitable and generous host. 'We shall have a full and merry house this Christmas', Dorothy confided to an old friend, ''Tis what the Duke delights in.' On the whole, however, he lived very moderately, confining his bouts of drinking to visits to his brother George at his Pavilion in Brighton. In August 1810 Mrs Jordan wrote with pursed lips to her son that the Duke had returned from Brighton complaining that he had been 'on very *hard duty* as to *drinking*'. In fact William had a remarkably strong head when he did indulge. Creevey recalled a drinking session hosted by the Prince of Wales at Brighton in which he and the Dukes of Clarence and Norfolk participated. Norfolk and Creevey both passed out, but the latter awoke to find the Prince of Wales and

68

his brother 'in a very animated discussion as to the particular shape and make of the wig worn by George II'.

Frequent interruptions to their seclusion at Bushy were Mrs Jordan's returns to the stage. Originally, her decision not to retire on striking up with William may have been partly motivated by her yearning for applause and the thrill of giving a good performance. There was, however, another, more practical consideration: she needed the money. The Duke, it is true, gave his mistress an income of £1,000 per annum, but she probably gave much of this to her daughters by previous associations. Her earnings were therefore an essential supplement to her income, and at times acted as a valuable increment to that of the Duke. For William was no economist; keeping within his income remained beyond him, and at times he gratefully availed himself of some of the ready cash earned by his mistress. He regarded these arrangements as purely temporary, punctiliously informing his banker, Coutts, of a loan of £420 from Mrs Jordan, and he was careful not to squander her money. In 1797 the Prince of Wales challenged him to an expensive wager, but William declined, pleading uprightly, 'Situated as I am with regard to Mrs Jordan, it would have been highly improper for me to have accepted your wager of five hundred guineas. However, I saw no harm in staking five.' Most of these loans were in fact repaid, some with interest, but gossip spread that William preyed greedily on the earnings of his mistress, and this gave rise to a malicious epigram:

> As Jordan's high and mighty squire
> Her playhouse profits deigns to skim
> Some folk audaciously enquire
> If *he* keeps her or *she* keeps him.

As the years went by, Dorothy derived less pleasure from her stage career, but her continued commitment to exhausting provincial tours was dictated not by the Duke's impatience to profit from her earnings but by her own determination to provide a generous dowry for her three eldest daughters by her previous lovers.

Her favourite role, however, remained that of matriarch, and indeed it was remarked that both she and the Duke were conscientious and loving parents. Even that malicious gossip,

69

A Cruikshank cartoon of 1792 deploring the treatment of the slaves on their passage across the Atlantic and calling for the abolition of the Slave Trade. William's impassioned defence of slavery before the House of Lords earned him much unpopularity in liberal circles.

Lord Glenbervie, was impressed when he saw William attending to his children at a party, and noted 'his care of these children and marked affection for them is certainly very amiable'. Indeed at times it seemed that the children were almost over indulged; they certainly could display wilfulness. Once Mrs Jordan added a postscript to a scribbled letter to the Duke: 'I desired George to put a kiss in this note – he immediately spit in it.'

William did not pass these years entirely withdrawn from public life. True, his pacifist speech of 1793 had infuriated not only his father but also the Prince of Wales, and as a result of severe admonitions from the royal family the Duke promised that in future he would refrain from censuring the Government in the House of Lords. He refused, however, to bridle his tongue elsewhere, and his immoderate abuse of Mr Pitt's Government, intemperately expressed to anyone who cared to listen, was considered positively scandalous. Nor did his circumspection in the Lords extend very far, for when non-political issues were discussed William felt fully competent to enter the debate. He was particularly vociferous in defence of the slave trade, believing that his service in the West Indies had endowed him with a rich insight into conditions pertaining in the plantations. The Duke was active in the debates of 1792, and in a speech of 1793 he robustly asserted that he believed the promoters of the Bill for abolition were either fanatics or hypocrites, 'and in one of those classes he ranked Mr Wilberforce'. He was later induced to apologize for this remark, but he remained staunch in defence, insisting, somewhat curiously, that 'the complexion of the slaves is the obstacle to every redress', and prophesying darkly that 'the slightest innovation will spread like flames over the sun burnt fields of a West Indian island'. These dire predictions today seem merely laughable, and indeed brought him some unpopularity at the time, but they were fairly representative of those who, although not especially reactionary or inhumane, sincerely believed that abolition would entail no benefit for humanity and could only bring economic collapse and social decline in its train. William's stance towards the slave trade demonstrates that, although at this time he was accounted a Whig, his political allegiance was determined more by a personal dislike of the Tory ministry headed by Pitt than by a coherently liberal viewpoint. He never shared the enthusiasm of those Whigs such as Fox who welcomed the French Revolution. Indeed, in 1792 he had written to Nelson, 'This pernicious and fallacious system of equality and universal liberty must be checked, or else we shall here have the most dreadful consequences.' But if William shied away from advanced political theories, he evinced in some debates in the Lords a certain common sense. In a debate on penalties for adultery he sensibly opposed the suggestion that no adulterer should be permitted to remarry; in another debate, discussing whether church attendances should be obligatory, he cogently argued that all compulsion in religious matters was fraught with danger. But his audience remained critical: it was felt to be unseemly that the King's son should display so intimate a knowledge of the subject of adultery, and his championship of optional church attendance sent the Archbishop of Canterbury scurrying in protest to King George. 'Very bad, very bad indeed!' agreed the King, 'I'll speak to Pitt about it.'

In 1801 Pitt resigned and was succeeded by Addington, but the new administration held its predecessors' low opinion of William's capabilities, and no offer of employment came his way. The Duke's contribution to public affairs remained confined to oratory in the House of Lords. But he took this

William Pitt, painted by Sir Thomas Lawrence. William's dislike for the Prime Minister stemmed from his belief that Pitt had encouraged his father to give him the most niggardly of allowances while he was a sea captain on service abroad. He was regrettably indiscreet in expressing his hostility towards Pitt, which did little to further his career.

preceding pages The House of Commons in 1793. William Pitt, standing, is making a speech and Charles James Fox is seated opposite him in the bottom row, fourth from left. The Tory administration headed by Pitt had no faith in William's capacities, and declined the Duke's repeated offers to serve his country in the struggle against France.

responsibility seriously. In 1803 he wrote gravely to a friend, 'In my opinion our ministers, and even the country, want energy, which I shall endeavour to give in every debate we have in Parliament', an undertaking one may feel sure he amply fulfilled. William was not even summoned from obscurity in 1810, when the King, overwhelmed by the death of his youngest daughter Amelia, sank into permanent derangement, necessitating the appointment of the Prince of Wales as Regent early in the following year. He signed a protest with the other royal dukes about the limitation of the Regent's powers, but even the removal of all such restrictions in 1812 did not presage the formation of a friendly Whig administration. To William's annoyance the Regent made only fitful approaches to his old allies, the Whigs, and they indignantly refused to participate in government on such terms. In February 1812 Mrs Jordan wrote to her son, 'The Prince has jilted all his old friends and I have some reason to think that your father is disappointed and very much *hurt*'. Certainly William remained a political nonentity, sulking on the fringes of opposition.

He did not, however, remain entirely detached from the upheavals of the Napoleonic Wars: in 1808 his son George was sent to join the army in Spain under Sir John Moore, and for the next six years he was frequently on campaign in the Peninsula. The Duke suffered agonies of indecision before agreeing to commit his fourteen-year-old son to so hazardous an enterprise, and in the ensuing years he was subject to the suspenseful distress that nags the parent of any soldier on active service. Mrs Jordan's anxiety was even more acute, but the Duke did his best to relieve her anguish: on one occasion he departed from Brighton at five in the morning so that he could join her at Bushy and share her misery as they waited to hear whether their son had been among the five thousand casualties sustained at the battle of Talavera in August 1809.

The bloody battle of Talavera of August 1809, at which William's illegitimate son George Fitzclarence served at the age of fifteen.

The Duke's failure to manage his own financial affairs perhaps indicates that it was in fact fortunate that he was not in charge of any concerns of greater import. In 1789 he had been endowed with an income of £12,000, increased in 1806 to £18,000, and occasionally this was supplemented by windfalls such as a dole from the Admiralty's hoard of prize money from captured ships. He found this insufficient and sought funds from other sources. In 1789 he had a relatively minor share in a loan raised by his two eldest brothers from bankers in the Hague, but like them he failed even to repay the interest. His banker friend Thomas Coutts helpfully lent him £20,000 for the refurbishment of Bushy, and Parliament also on one occasion obliged him with a loan of £30,000, although in 1804 there were awkward questions in the house about the Duke's failure to make the agreed repayments of £750 a quarter. In 1796 the Elector of Hesse Cassel lent him £12,000 – and, besides, he had occasional recourse to Mrs Jordan. It was not enough, however, and his debts merely piled higher. As his children grew older they involved him in fresh expense. George Fitzclarence, for example, was prone to extravagance, ordering quantities of useless items to take abroad, and thoughtlessly running up debts. 'I am aware that your uniform is expensive, that you are with young officers who care not for money', William wrote in understanding if weary reproach, promising to try and settle his son's bills if he forswore gaming houses and the turf. In the face of these accumulating worries the Duke began to consider adopting the drastic solution of abandoning Mrs Jordan and contracting himself in marriage to an heiress.

This vague scheme assumed real significance when, on 19 June 1811, the Duke met the attractive and wealthy Miss Catherine Tylney-Long at a fête at Carlton House to which Mrs Jordan had not been invited. Miss Long was reputed to be worth £40,000 a year, and having thought the matter over for some months William became determined to make a bid for her hand. Meanwhile the unwitting Mrs Jordan had set out on yet another provincial tour, apparently with no conception of her imminent dismissal. In early October she was due to perform at Cheltenham when a letter from the Duke was delivered, requesting that she should proceed to Maidenhead to discuss terms of separation. With true professionalism she tried to

Tickets Delivered by

Mr. STEVENS,

BOX-OFFICE-KEEPER,

Will be Admitted this Evening.

Mrs. JORDAN's Fifth Night.

Theatre-Royal, Richmond-Green,

FRIDAY, September 2, 1796,

Will be prefented, a COMEDY, (in two Acts,) call'd

The WEDDING DAY.

Lord Rakeland   by   Mr.   WELLS,

Mr. Milden Mr. MADDOCKS,   Mr. Conteft Mr. PHILLIPS

Sir Adam Conteft   by   Mr.   WILLIAMS,

Lady Autumn   by   Mrs.   BENSON,

Mrs. Hamford Mrs. MILLS,   Hannah Mifs SMYTH

And the Part of Lady CONTEST by

Mrs. JORDAN.

After which will be performed a FARCE, call'd

THE VIRGIN UNMASK'D

Goodwill   by   Mr.   DAVENPORT,

Coupee Mr. WILLIAMS,   Quaver Mr. PHILLIPS,

Blifter Mr. SHAW,   Thomas Mr. BLURTON,

And the Part of Mifs LUCY by

Mrs. JORDAN

To which will be added, the Farce of

The SULTAN.

Solyman   by   Mr.   CLAREMONT,

Mutes by Meff. BLURTON and CURTIS,

Ofmyn   by   Mr.   WILLIAMS,

Elmira   by   Mifs   SMYTH,

Ifmena   by   Mifs   WALCUP,

And the Part of ROXALANA by

rs. JORDAN.

Tickets to be had of Mr. STEVENS, near *Richmond-Bridge.*

Mrs Jordan on stage on the night that she learnt the Duke of Clarence was leaving her. Although required by the script to roar with laughter Dorothy was so distressed that instead she burst into tears.

honour her engagement on the stage that evening, but hardly surprisingly her performance lacked much of its usual spontaneous gaiety. At one point the script called for her to burst into irrepressible laughter, but instead of her celebrated joyous peals she broke into tempestuous sobs. The rest of the cast helped her struggle through the final act, and then, still clad in her stage costume, she clambered tearfully into her coach to keep her distressing appointment with the Duke. At Maidenhead she nobly agreed that arrangements for a separation should proceed.

Mrs Jordan had no doubts about the reasons for this estrangement. 'Money, money, my good friend, or the want of it, has, I am convinced, made HIM at this moment the most wretched of men', she lamented to a trusted confidant, adding

78

forgivingly, 'With all his excellent qualities, his domestic *virtues*, his love for his *lovely* children, what must he not at this moment suffer?' Certainly the underlying explanation for the breach *was* a financial one, but there may have been other considerations lurking at the back of the Duke's mind. Arduous years of childbearing had taken their toll on Mrs Jordan's neat figure, which Hazlitt noted had of late become 'large, soft and generous like her soul'. The prospect of a somewhat younger partner might well have seemed appealing to the Duke. William had seen his mother more often than usual since the advent of his father's final decline in 1810, and perhaps she had urged him to abandon his concubine. In addition, he might have nourished hopes of producing a legitimate heir who could reign in Hanover, a throne from which the Regent's daughter, Princess Charlotte, was debarred by virtue of Salic law.

Mrs Jordan was determined that the parting should be amicable, and after a brief wrangle over the arrangements made for her provision a settlement was drawn up in January 1812 with which she declared herself 'perfectly satisfied', and which William himself felt was conclusive testimony that he could 'justly value the conduct of a lady for twenty years'. She was to be given an annual allowance of £1,500, together with £600 towards a house and coach and £800 for her daughters by Daly and Ford. An additional £1,500 was provided for the maintenance of her youngest daughters, but it was stated that, in the event of Mrs Jordan returning to the stage, she would forfeit both this sum and the custody of her daughters, a somewhat harsh stipulation considering there had been no objection to Dorothy performing while she contributed to the Duke's pocket. Nevertheless, she bravely accepted these terms, moved out of Bushy and installed herself in a house in Cadogan Place.

Her retirement was neither untroubled nor prolonged. Sophia Fitzclarence, her eldest daughter by the Duke, callously ignored her mother following the separation from her father, cutting her even when they met in public. Then Thomas Alsop, the husband of her daughter Frances fathered by Richard Daly, became involved in debt, and she felt it her duty to return to her career to earn money to satisfy his creditors. Her youngest daughters were promptly removed from Cadogan Place, and, although she was still permitted to have occasional access to them, the loss of their company caused her deep distress. In 1814 George and Henry Fitzclarence, by now both serving in the Peninsula, were disgraced on account of their unsuccessful attempt to have their superior officer court-martialled, and the Regent decreed that they should be exiled to the army in India. Worst of all, Frederick March, the husband of one of her daughters by Richard Ford, grievously defrauded her, and by 1815 she found herself heavily in debt. In a panic she applied for advice to the Duke's man of business, John Barton, who appears never to have revealed to his master the true extent of her difficulties. Anxious to prevent unfavourable publicity, he apparently encouraged her to flee to France, promising to sort out her affairs discreetly in her absence. This he lamentably failed to do, and the unfortunate actress languished in a squalid apartment at St Cloud, forlornly strumming on a guitar while anxiously waiting for letters from England. The strain was too much for her already feeble health: she collapsed on 5 July 1816 and died three days later. The Duke was distressed to hear of her death and indignant with those he conceived responsible: 'The infamy and rascality of March and Mrs Alsop . . . will prevent my further intercourse with them', he wrote to his son George, but in fact he himself cannot be absolved from all blame for the tragedy. Mrs Jordan had been a devoted mistress and mother, selfishly discarded after twenty years, and his consideration for her welfare should have extended further than the mere regular payment of her pension.

In fact, far from being 'the most wretched of men', the Duke, upon his separation from Mrs Jordan, had thrown himself into his courtship of Miss Long with remarkable zest. He pursued her down to Ramsgate, and really fancied himself in love with 'the lovely little nice angel'. He was optimistic about his chances, for her family encouraged his attentions and he felt convinced that the Regent would give his consent to the match. 'If I was younger and knew less of the world I should flatter myself she was really in love with me', he confided to her aunt, but although Miss Long was indeed in love it was not with William. The rakishly attractive William Wellesley Pole lurked persistently by her side, and despite the Duke's clumsy attempts to shoo him away it soon became clear where 'the bewitching Catherine's' own preferences lay. William recovered swiftly from this setback: even before Miss Long's betrothal to Pole was formally announced he was in hot pursuit of other eligible ladies. In swift succession he unsuccessfully proposed to the dowager Lady Downshire, Miss Margaret Mercer Elphinstone and Lady Berkeley, while society looked on in bemusement at this swapping of partners more akin to a rumbustious country dance than to accepted ideas of formal courtship. The wags even prophesied that the Willises, the quack doctors who looked after mad King George, would shortly have another patient in need of their attentions.

Spurned by the English ladies, Clarence considered a more exotic spouse. At the end of 1813 he decided to offer himself to the Duchess of Oldenburgh, the twenty-five-year-old widowed sister of Tsar Alexander I. In January 1814 he set off to Holland to meet her, a mission financed by the Regent. Despite this monetary aid, his relations with the Grand Duchess were not destined to prosper. In March 1814 the Duke escorted her across the Channel on a visit to England, but there she confided to Princess Charlotte that she abhorred his vulgar familiarity, and dismissed him as 'awkward, not without wit, but definitely unpleasant'.

With this rejection, the frenzied pace of William's courtships slackened. He declined to marry his cousin Princess Sophia of Gloucester, and although he toyed with the idea of approaching the eldest daughter of the Landgrave of Hesse, the urgency had gone out of the chase. He busied himself with minor duties of state ceremonial, ferrying the restored King Louis XVIII to France, and conducting the King of Prussia and the Tsar across the Channel after their visit to England, startling them somewhat with his bad language. The prospect of marriage receded into the distance; bachelordom seemed quite palatable after all. Perhaps, indeed, the Duke agreed with the Regent that it was unlikely that anyone would accept him. For the moment there seemed no good reason to disturb his placid existence.

The Duchess of Oldenburgh, the widowed sister of Tsar Alexander I, whom William hoped to wed. She rejected his suit, dismissing the Duke as 'awkward, not without wit, but definitely unpleasant'.

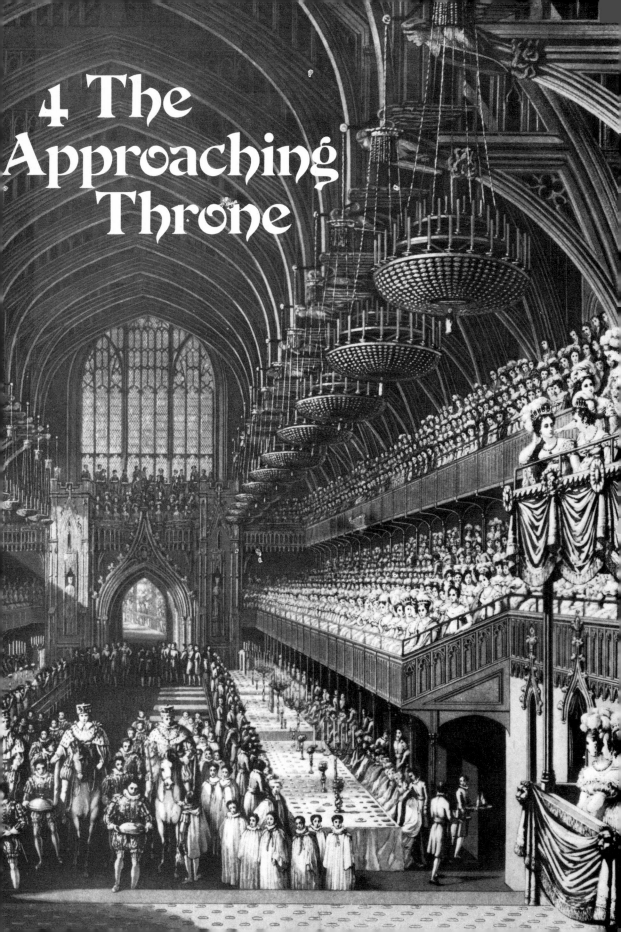

4 The Approaching Throne

IN 1816 THE REGENT'S ONLY CHILD, Princess Charlotte, had married Prince Leopold of Saxe-Coburg, and soon she became pregnant. As the Princess neared her confinement, the prospect of William succeeding to the throne must have seemed increasingly remote. No complications were expected at the birth, and the Duke of Clarence accompanied his mother to Bath, where she planned to take the waters to fortify her for the arrival of her first great-grandchild. On 19 November 1817 news arrived that the Princess had been delivered of a dead child, but that she herself was doing well. There seemed no cause for serious alarm, and after some hesitation William agreed that, as planned, he should attend a banquet in the Pump Room at Bath. While there, he received a momentous communication: due to unforeseen difficulties Princess Charlotte had died in the aftermath of childbirth.

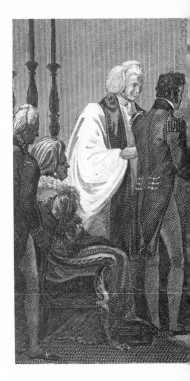

William had been fond of his niece, but inevitably it could not have been the purely personal aspect of the tragedy that struck him most forcibly, for only the bulky forms of his two elder brothers now stood between him and the throne. There

above The marriage of Princess Charlotte to Leopold of Saxe-Coburg. At the ceremony William gave away his niece.

left The funeral of Princess Charlotte, daughter of George IV. Her death meant that the Hanoverian line was in danger of dying out and necessitated the marriage of the bachelor princes in the hope that one of them would produce an heir to the throne.

preceding pages George IV's coronation was followed by celebrations characterized by the most lavish extravagance, such as this banquet for all the peers of the realm. William's own coronation was a much simpler affair.

was, furthermore, the future of the dynasty to consider, for the House of Brunswick, once so populous, seemed in danger of permanent extinction. The Duke of York had married in 1791, but the marriage had proved barren, and although William's younger brother the unpopular Duke of Cumberland had in 1815 married his saucy cousin, he too remained childless as yet. William's three other younger brothers had never legally married, and even his youngest surviving sister, Princess Sophia, was approaching the end of her childbearing days. Clearly, measures had to be taken to ensure the eventual appearance of an heir to continue the line, and the marriage of the bachelor Princes was an essential prerequisite. William must be prodded into doing his duty to the nation; Princess Elizabeth wrote significantly, 'The Queen will talk to William'. However, the Duke, formerly so eager to marry, now found himself assailed by doubts. He was fearful that some strange Princess selected as his bride would not welcome a constant reminder in the shape of the Fitzclarences of his liaison with Mrs Jordan, and that his access to his children would be hindered. Furthermore, the ladies to whom he had previously proposed had all been wealthy, but the prospect of a generous dowry accompanying a northern Princess seemed remote. Accordingly, in December 1817, he wrote to Queen Charlotte outlining his doubts, insisting that if the Cabinet thought it necessary for him to marry they must reveal what arrangements they intended for his financial provision; stressing that with debts totalling £56,000, ten children entirely dependent on him and himself 'turned *fifty*, it would' he wrote, 'be madness in me to marry without previously knowing what my income would be'. He added that once pecuniary matters had been settled a further difficulty remained outstanding, for he would have to explain his '*real* situation as the fond and attached father of ten children'; he trenchantly concluded, 'without a *complete* understanding of my determination to see my daughters when and where I please I cannot and will not marry.' Queen Charlotte, however, was sanguine that no 'reasonable princess' could object to William seeing his children, provided they had a separate establishment, and the Prime Minister, Lord Liverpool, at first seemed very accommodating over the question of finance, promising that William's income would be increased to £40,000, which

The Prime Minister, Lord Liverpool. At first he promised that William would enjoy a substantially increased income on his marriage, but political considerations subsequently forced him to be less generous.

would include a provision for his five daughters. Accordingly, the Duke agreed to make a bid for the hand of the younger daughter of the King of Denmark, but she, appalled by the discrepancy in their ages, hastily pleaded that she was not yet of an age to be separated from her parents, 'for which I much admire her', said William generously.

The Duke's gallant reaction was not, in fact, entirely selfless. Even while negotiations with the Danish court were in progress William had espied another English heiress who seemed worthy of his attentions. Miss Wyckham (an heiress dismissed rather unkindly by Greville as half crazy) had inherited through her grandmother Lord Wenman's estate in Oxfordshire; she

86

enjoyed an exciting reputation for unconventionality, being apparently in the habit of donning spurs and leaping five-barred gates. William found this combination of wealth and eccentricity irresistible and in February 1818 he proposed, this time successfully. It soon emerged though that William was still bound by the shackles of the Royal Marriage Act, and when he heard from the Regent, who did not approve of the match, that it was improbable he would secure the consent of Parliament William and his fiancée sadly agreed to break off the engagement. He was genuinely distressed by this outcome, writing brokenly to his son George, 'At present I think and exist only for Miss Wyckham', but he patriotically agreed to co-operate in the search for a spouse of whom Parliament could approve. An application for the hand of the nineteen-year-old daughter of the Electoral Prince of Hesse Cassel was rejected; but William's young brother the Duke of Cambridge, who was acting as his emissary, continued to scour the foreign courts in a persistent effort to furnish his brother with a mate. He finally happened upon the tiny state of Saxe-Meiningen, where the widowed Duchess promptly accepted a proposal on behalf of her twenty-six-year-old daughter Adelaide. On 21 March William wrote to his son George Fitzclarence in a mood of dutiful gloom, informing him of the identity of his new stepmother: 'It is to be the Princess of Saxe-Meiningen, whose *beauty* and *character* are universally acknowledged. She is doomed, *poor, dear, innocent, young* creature to be *my* wife. I *cannot*, I *will not*, I *must not* ill use her ...' The Duke was shaken from this fit of mournful rumination by an unpleasant financial jolt. Lord Liverpool, nervously aware that Parliament was in no mood to countenance excessive public expenditure, reduced the proposed increase to William's income to £10,000 a year. Even so, the House of Commons, gleeful at an opportunity for revenge on one of those royal dukes whom the Duke of Wellington claimed had '*personally* insulted two thirds of the gentlemen of England', slashed it still further to £6,000. William haughtily informed the House that such an increase was so irrelevant to his needs that he would not even deign to accept it, and for a time it seemed that his marriage might be abandoned altogether. Adelaide, however, remained prepared to press on with the match and, upon reconsideration, the Duke too decided that the

William's younger brother
Edward, Duke of Kent,
father of Queen Victoria.
He died in January 1820,
before his daughter's first
birthday.

reports of the Princess's amiable character warranted persever-
ance. A suitable wife who would tolerate his illegitimate
offspring was too rare a creature to be lightly dismissed, and he
reflected, besides, that a renewed feminine influence at Bushy
would be very welcome for it had become infinitely less
homely since the departure of Mrs Jordan.

Nevertheless, William displayed little of the ardour conven-
tionally associated with a triumphant suitor. Unlike his brother
the Duke of Kent, who rushed off to Germany personally to
escort his prospective bride to England, William remained
firmly at home while Princess Adelaide and her mother gamely

88

accomplished the journey on their own. They arrived in London on the evening of 4 July 1818, and installed themselves in Grillon's Hotel, where they waited nervously in their apartments until the Regent finally paid them a late night visit, followed at last by the bridegroom himself.

The marriage ceremony was conducted at Kew Palace on 13 July and attended by the ailing Queen. The marriage of the Duke and Duchess of Kent was celebrated simultaneously; after the service the couples repaired for a family feast in the company of the Regent before William, Adelaide and the bride's mother journeyed back to London, the newlyweds no doubt nervously eyeing one another as they made strained conversation in the jolting coach.

There was perhaps little in Adelaide's outward appearance to reassure on first inspection, although her bearing and deportment had a certain grace that somewhat compensated for her plain features. Lady Bedingfield wrote that 'her manner is found pleasing but she is not handsome', while Lady Granville frankly described her as 'ugly', but added that she had 'a good tournure and manner'. If, however, her physical endowments were slight, her character was of sterling worth, for beneath her shyly unassuming air was a capacity for affection, kindness and loyalty, a devotion to duty and an upstanding morality of truly impressive proportions. Perhaps, indeed, it was the very excess of her goodness that irked the cynical and sophisticated court society of the time, unable to believe that anyone so utterly admirable could be anything other than a nonentity. Fashionable ladies such as Lady Jersey snubbed her and Princess Sophia gave her the malicious sobriquet of 'Mrs Aquatic', but in fact her many excellent qualities were bolstered by a latent streak of obstinacy resulting overall in a far from negligible character. Her influence on William was almost wholly good, and the Duke, overcome with relief that, although no beauty, this mystery German Princess should prove so truly good natured and companionable, swiftly settled to become the most uxorious of husbands. Under her guidance his language and manners improved immeasurably. A guest at a dinner which William attended was amazed at the change which a very few years of married life had wrought in his bearing: throughout the meal, he reported, William 'behaved perfectly well, was civil to

everybody, even gentlemanlike in character, did not say a single indecent or improper thing'.

Soon after the wedding the couple departed for Hanover. William's indignant rejection of Parliament's offer of a meagre increase to his income meant that he could not afford to retire to Bushy and quietly pursue the life of a prosperous country gentleman. A spell on the Continent, where the cost of living was lower than at home, was imperative if the Duke's finances were to be restored to order. They were welcomed in Hanover by the Duke of Cambridge, at that time Governor-General of the province and also newly married. Cambridge cheerfully relayed to his family the news that William and Adelaide already seemed devoted to each other, and it soon appeared that the success of the marriage was to be clinched by the arrival of a child.

opposite Adelaide of Saxe Meiningen, William's bride. Although never a great beauty, she was an eminently suitable wife for the Duke.

Adolphus, Duke of Cambridge, William's youngest brother. He was Governor-General of Hanover when the Duke and Duchess of Clarence went to live there.

The widowed Duchess of Kent and her daughter Princess Victoria.

In November 1818 William proudly reported home that the Duchess was pregnant, and for the next few months he waited anxiously for the appearance of a new heir to the throne. Then a neglected cold of Adelaide's developed into pleurisy, and the course of bleeding prescribed by the doctors provoked the premature birth of a baby daughter. Charlotte Augusta survived for less than a day before her tiny corpse was interred by the side of the body of King George I. Adelaide's life was also feared for for some days. 'I trust this amiable little Duchess will soon recover her strength', wrote the Dowager Queen of Wurtenberg in concern. 'By all accounts she is the very woman calculated to suit my dear William's taste and he loves her very

92

much.' Fortunately the Duchess rallied, and by early August 1819 William could diffidently confide to Lord Liverpool that he had 'every reason to believe that the Duchess is once more with child'. This time, he determined, the child should be born in England, and accordingly they set out on their journey home, paying visits *en route* to William's sisters in Hesse Homburg and Wurtenberg and Adelaide's sister in Ghent. Hardly surprisingly, this arduous round of social activities, combined with the strains of early nineteenth-century travel, was too much for Adelaide's delicate constitution, and in September 1819 she miscarried at Calais.

Safely back in England, there was little time to brood on this misfortune, for other family matters intruded to distract the Clarences. In January 1820 the Duke of Kent died unexpectedly, leaving behind a widow and a little daughter, Victoria. Soon afterwards poor mad King George succumbed also, and

King George III as an old man. The death of Princess Amelia caused the King's permanent derangement, and he lived in seclusion until his death in 1820.

93

on 31 January 1820, the Regent, who had for so long been King in all but name, was proclaimed King George IV. He embarked on his reign in a vengeful frame of mind, concentrating his energies on a bid to rid himself of his outrageous wife, Caroline of Brunswick. William wholeheartedly supported his brother in this campaign. Indeed, Lord Brougham, who was acting as Caroline's counsel, actually asserted that William had attempted to engineer her disgrace by urging a naval officer to seduce her, but while it is improbable that William would have had either the guile or lack of scruple to dream up such a stratagem, he left no doubt where his loyalties lay. Mr Creevey reported that when the Duke's name was called at the final reading in the Lords of the Bill of Pains and Penalties against the Queen, 'he leaned over the rail of the gallery as far into the house as he could and halloed "content" with a yell that would have quite become a savage'.

opposite, above Princess Caroline of Brunswick, eccentric wife of George IV, whom he sought to divorce at the beginning of his reign.

opposite, below The trial of Queen Caroline in the House of Lords. During the debate on the Bill of Pains and Penalties William noisily signified his support for his eldest brother. Nevertheless George IV failed in his attempt to rid himself of the wife he abhorred.

left Sir Thomas Lawrence's portrait of Henry Brougham, who acted as Caroline's counsel during her trial. He claimed, improbably, that William had attempted to discredit his sister-in-law by arranging for her seduction.

His own marriage, however, continued to thrive, and in December 1820 it seemed that his patience had been rewarded when the Duchess presented him with a fine girl, proudly christened Elizabeth. The child took the breast with heartening vigour, but these encouraging signs were deceptive, for on 4 March 1821 she died of inflammation of the bowels, leaving her parents inconsolable. His hopes rose once more the following year when Adelaide conceived again, and her solicitous husband reported that she seemed in better health than in her previous pregnancies. The impression was misleading, for in April 1822 she again miscarried, this time of twins. 'I want words to express my feelings at these repeated misfortunes to this beloved and superior woman', wrote William to his brother in the deepest distress; 'I am quite broken hearted'. It began to seem improbable that Adelaide could provide William with a longed-for heir; little Victoria's pre-eminence remained unchallenged. To their great credit, neither of them ever evinced any resentment against their bouncingly healthy niece. On the contrary, their attitude was uniformly generous. Adelaide wrote touchingly to the Duchess of Kent, 'My children are dead but your child lives, and she is mine too.' Yet little Victoria could not adequately compensate for their own empty nursery, and their childlessness was particularly hard to bear in view of the fact that they both had a natural aptitude for communicating with children. In 1822 Adelaide wrote a delightful letter to the little Princess, concluding 'Uncle William and Aunt Adelaide also beg little Victoria to give dear Mama, and dear Sissi a kiss in their name and to Aunt Augusta . . . and the Big Doll.'

Throughout these years William and Adelaide paid intermittent visits to continental spas in the hope that the springs would boost the Duchess's fertility. Gradually, however, disillusion became complete: years later, when King, William was heard to gruffly mutter 'Damn'd stuff' on reading a newspaper report that his wife was pregnant once again.

Although his failure to produce a legitimate heir was a source of lasting disappointment to William, there was at least the enormous brood of Fitzclarences to offer him consolation. Their ranks had been depleted in early 1818 when Henry Fitzclarence, serving with his brother George in the army in

Princess Victoria, aged ten. William and Adelaide were both dotingly fond of children and were anxious to lavish affection on their niece.

India, had been struck down by fever, but to compensate for this grievous loss George now hastened home to England. His fond father was living in Hanover at the time and considered appointing him his equerry, only to receive a heavy hint from the Regent that such a move would demonstrate a certain lack of delicacy towards the sensibilities of his new wife. William treated the suggestion with scorn. 'No one has a higher respect for the character of *wife* than *myself*', he wrote defiantly, 'and I esteem from the bottom of my heart the *excellent* and *sensible* Princess I have married and I will never *lower* her in any manner; but I again repeat *no earthly* power *shall prevent* my seeing *where* and *how* I choose my children and my making George my equerry.' In point of fact the appointment was never made, but not on account of Adelaide's opposition for it soon emerged that she was a model stepmother, displaying a remarkable breadth of vision on the subject of the Duke's former mistress. Before her arrival at Bushy, William, with uncharacteristic if somewhat elementary tact, had removed a portrait of Mrs Jordan from its place of honour in the drawing-room, but on hearing of its removal Adelaide instructed that it should be returned, sensing that William would feel more comfortable. Although William's daughters were established in a house in South Audley Street, Adelaide regularly entertained the whole family at Bushy, and George Fitzclarence had no hesitation in proclaiming her 'the best woman in the world'. The Fitzclarences, however, were already showing signs of that overweening arrogance which was to be their distinguishing feature in later years. In society parlance they were collectively known as *Les Batards*, and their pretensions were already the subject of unfavourable comment. In March 1821 Lady Williams-Wynn wrote of the death of the Clarences' daughter Elizabeth, 'I couldn't help feeling sorry for our poor Queen Bess, though I could not bear the degree of rank that the Fitzclarences had taken on her birth.' The elder Fitzclarences were now of an age to wed, and their marriages provided William with a steady stream of grandchildren who served to enliven his advancing middle age.

If William did not emerge from his marriage sensibly enriched, the fact that the prudent Adelaide now took charge of his expenses ensured that his burden of debt became less

Adelaide much
appreciated the simplicity
of life at Bushy, where she
could entertain informally.

oppressive. In 1821 William swallowed his pride and applied to
Parliament for the increase in income which he had previously
so disdainfully rejected; as he was awarded the backlog of
payment due to him, this made quite a tidy endowment. His
financial pressures were further eased in 1823 when George IV
arranged for him to have a profitable sinecure in the Marines,
and soon his position had improved to the degree that he felt it
possible to start work on a sumptuous new London residence.
'Billy Clarence . . . is rigging up in a small way in the stable
yard', Mr Creevey noted somewhat patronizingly in 1826; but
certainly Clarence House, which resulted from these activities,
was an infinitely more imposing habitation than his previous
cramped apartments at St James's Palace.

Despite this impressive new domicile, William remained at
his happiest in the more informal surroundings of Bushy.

98

Visitors to the house reported that there was a refreshing lack of etiquette, the principal amusements being friendly games of cards and strolls round the garden and farm. The contrast between the simplicity of their lifestyle and that pertaining in George IV's Pavilion at Brighton was startling; the Clarences were so unaccustomed to rich food and self-indulgence that a visit to the Pavilion in 1823 resulted in Adelaide suffering from stomach pains and William being laid low with gout. With his habitual moderation it is hardly surprising that William enjoyed blooming health, suffering only from occasional asthmatic attacks, an affliction which he bore with tolerance and good humour.

In 1827 William's prospects for the future underwent a dramatic change. Frederick, the Duke of York, who had always expected to outlive his brother George, had sunk into a decline the previous year, and on 7 January 1827 he finally died. Only now did it appear inevitable that William would succeed to the throne. It was a thought that apparently failed to enthral the King, who, although fond of William, held no high opinion of his intellect. 'Look at that idiot!' he allegedly exclaimed to Princess Lieven over dinner one day; 'They will remember me, if ever he is in my place.' William himself entertained no such lack of confidence in his own abilities. The Duke of York's funeral was conducted in freezing temperatures which were accounted responsible for the deaths of several of the frailer mourners. William, however, was in the grip of warm elation. He behaved most indecorously throughout the service, and was periodically heard to remark to the Duke of Sussex, 'We shall be treated *now* brother Augustus, very differently from what we have been'. However unsuitable the remark, it contained much truth: at the funeral it was noted that many peers who invariably ignored the Duke of Clarence now paid him deferential attention. An additional bonus of his new position of heir to the throne was that he received an augmentation of £12,000 to his income.

Then, in February 1827, the Prime Minister, Lord Liverpool, was discovered prostrate in his breakfast-room, his political career terminated by a severe stroke. In April George Canning was requested by the King to form an administration, an invitation he found some difficulty in fulfilling as many established politicians distrusted him too much to serve under him. Scrabbling round for support, Canning decided his hand would be strengthened if he could give an indication that the heir to the throne was solidly behind him. Accordingly he determined to appoint William to the position of Lord High Admiral, a sonorously titled post more redolent to modern ears of comic opera than power politics, and which had indeed remained unoccupied since the days of Queen Anne, whose husband had been the last incumbent. The appointment was hailed as an inspired move on Canning's part by some political observers: 'Nothing served so much to discomfort his opponents', Mr Greville noted sagaciously, but some regarded the prospect of William in so elevated a position with a marked degree of alarm. 'It is not a light thing to place an almost irresponsible person at the head of a department with so immense an expenditure as the navy', remarked Mr Hobhouse with concern. The Government, on the other hand, felt confident that the terms set out in William's letter of appointment would prevent him from holding too unlimited a sway over naval affairs: it was clearly stated that the Lord High Admiral's Council must authorize his policy decisions and that two members of his Council should accompany him when at sea. The appointment was also wise for reasons other than political expediency, for since William might have been called at any time to the throne it was desirable that he should gain a measure of experience in public affairs. Indeed, although it turned out that the checks on William's authority were insufficient to ensure the success of his assignment, his experiences as Lord High Admiral were of crucial significance in helping him to deal with the larger responsibilities of kingship. Anyway, Canning did not survive to witness the consequences of his appointment: in August 1827 he died, briefly succeeded as Premier by Goderich before the Duke of Wellington ushered in a Tory administration.

At first it seemed that William would thrive in his new position, for his access to office was marked by a flow of cordiality. He genially requested that all members of the existing Admiralty Council should stay in office and assist him with his new responsibilities, and expressed delight on hearing that he was expected to entertain in his official capacity. He

busied himself sailing round the southern ports, while Adelaide, who had no stomach for the sea, followed him over land in order to attend the receptions he hosted in the evenings. Unfortunately William did not confine himself to hospitality and speechifying. By day he energetically poked into the corners of the dockyards, investigating abuses and proposing remedies. The Government and his Council began to fear that he would not be the passive instrument of their policy which

The Duke of Wellington, who as Prime Minister had to deal with William in his capacity as Lord High Admiral.

they had envisaged. The Duke of Wellington tactfully submitted that William's exhausting devotion to duty might undermine his health, a suggestion which William cheerfully refuted. 'The eye of the Lord High Admiral does infinite good', he gravely insisted, a maxim which the Government was to find increasingly dubious.

One source of potential confusion in the determination of naval policy lay in William's belief that he was above the petty demands of party intrigue, and that he was only required to perform his duty, 'without waiting the cold calculation of political considerations'. When Admiral Codrington, stationed in the Eastern Mediterranean, destroyed the Turkish Fleet at Navarino in October 1827 without the explicit authority of the Admiralty, William felt no inhibitions in expressing his belief that the victory redounded to the glory of Britain. The rumour that he had actually encouraged Codrington by writing to him 'Go in, My dear Ned and smash these Turks' was unfounded, but certainly on hearing the news of the battle William wrote in enthusiastic praise to the Admiral, and persuaded George IV to make arrangements for a dispensation of honours and promotions for the officers involved that was quite unprecedented in naval history. But the Government took a cooler view of the matter: William's championship of Codrington could not prevent his recall, and in the King's speech of January 1828 Navarino was referred to as 'this untoward event'. It already seemed evident that there was a disturbing split in outlook between William and the ministers.

It was, however, in the realm of naval administration that trouble really loomed. Cheerfully ignoring the terms of his appointment William conceived of his Council as a purely advisory body, but unfortunately the Council, headed by the arrogantly conservative Sir George Cockburn, was in no mood to tolerate the infringement of its prerogatives. William was determined to inaugurate a series of penetrating reforms within the system, and with this in mind he established a committee on gunnery and imperiously summoned its members to discuss the issue with him at Portsmouth. Sir George Cockburn protested at what he conceived as William's unwarranted interference in matters beyond his scope. A hot exchange of letters ensued, culminating in William demanding that Sir George should be

opposite The controversial Admiral Codrington at the battle of Navarino. In attacking the Turkish Fleet Codrington had been acting largely on his own initiative, and his victory caused much embarrassment to the British Government. William, however, was an enthusiastic supporter of Codrington's action.

dismissed. The Duke of Wellington was not prepared to comply with this injunction, particularly as he was aware that Cockburn would take his entire Council with him if he left, and he enlisted the support of the King to deal with his recalcitrant brother. On 15 July 1828 George wrote sorrowfully to William, 'It is with feelings of deep regret that I observe the embarrassing situation in which you have placed yourself. You are in error from beginning to end. This is not a matter of opinion, it is a positive fact . . . I love you *most truly* as you know, and no one would do more or go further to protect and meet your feelings; but on the present occasion I have no alternative; you must give way and listen to the affection of your best friend and most attached brother.' Unnerved by this communication, William did patch up a paltry sort of reconciliation with Sir George on 18 July. The peace could not endure. While on yet another inspection of outlying ports, William came across a squadron of ships waiting for the arrival of Admiral Blackwood. Without more ado he hoisted his flag in his yacht the *Royal Sovereign*, and gleefully ordered the two three-deckers and other smaller vessels to follow him out to sea. He remained afloat till 4 August, while wild rumours circulated London about the whereabouts of both himself and the fleet. Lord Ellenborough revealed details to a correspondent: 'No one knows where the Lord High Admiral is gone . . . he has ordered pilots . . . the orders are to be secret.' It was even claimed that he planned to take the squadron to Copenhagen so that George Fitzclarence could have an opportunity to see it.

William returned to London on 7 August, not at all abashed at the implications of his irresponsible jaunt, and he unconcernedly resumed his abusive feud with Sir George Cockburn. Wellington, however, felt that the Duke's behaviour impelled his intervention. He sent the Lord High Admiral a severe admonition, and on 9 August he 'had a violent scene with him' which culminated in William offering to resign unless he was given a freer hand in naval policy. Wellington communicated this to the King, who wearily gave his verdict on the matter. 'I love my brother William, I have always done so to my heart's core, and I will leave him the example of what the inherent duty of a king of this country really is', he wrote to Wellington on 11 August; but he pithily concluded, 'The Lord High Admiral shall strictly obey the laws enacted by Parliament as attached to his present station or I desire immediately to receive his resignation.' William elected to resign rather than submit to such constraint. Accordingly on 14 August he announced his decision to his Council, darkly muttering that if he had not regarded himself as bound by his obligations as a military officer he would have had much to say on the subject of his departure. However, on being told that his whole Council would have resigned if Cockburn had been dismissed, William behaved with great magnanimity, shaking hands with Sir George and inviting him and his other enemies to attend his birthday party at Bushy the following week. Nor did he bear a grudge against Wellington, for he confided to a friend that 'he could not help admiring the clearness and straightforwardness with which he had conducted himself to him as heir presumptive to the throne'.

William's failure in office derived more from his inability to manage people than from the intrinsic idiocy of his policies. The reforms he managed to enact nearly all had merit. He modified the anachronistic system of promotion, criticized the lamentable state of naval gunnery and restricted the use of flogging, and in general showed himself capable of piercing the layers of complacency and conservatism which clogged the effective functioning of the Navy. Convinced, however, that all opposition to his policies resulted from selfish obstinacy, he lacked the skill of a politician in manipulating recalcitrant colleagues. His experience at the Admiralty at least partially impressed upon him that a frontal assault on entrenched positions did not guarantee their collapse.

For the next two years William waited in the wings of power, occasionally emerging into the spotlight in his supporting role as heir to the throne. In 1829 he supported the Wellington Government's Bill for Catholic Emancipation. His stance on emancipation had in the past been inconsistent: in 1820 he had told the Duke of Norfolk, debarred as a catholic from sitting in the House of Lords, that he hoped to see him soon in that assembly; but he voted against emancipation in 1821. This apparent hypocrisy was in part dictated by deference to the anti-catholic views of the Duke of York, but now he considered that York's death left him a free agent. In February

ANOTHER MISTAKE !!!

POOR BILLY

1829 he rose to speak in defence of the measure, somewhat to the alarm of the Bill's supporters who feared he would say something 'violent and foolish' and undermine their cause. In fact he made a very tolerable if somewhat verbose speech, although admittedly getting rather carried away in the subsequent exchanges of debate and subjecting his reactionary brother the Duke of Cumberland to the most unmeasured abuse. His support of the Bill was popular with the public at large and gained for him the image of a tolerant liberal, an agreeable new experience for the Duke.

By early 1830 it had become clear that the health of the King was steadily deteriorating. William had always been devoted to his brother, and his sympathy for his final sufferings was genuine. He paid regular visits to the King and always returned 'crying like a child'. Yet as the throne loomed ever larger a note of excitement mingled with his distress. He could not restrain himself from despatching letters to Wellington assuring him that he meant to retain him in office upon his accession, communications of a quite unconstitutional nature which Wellington very properly ignored. The King himself certainly resented what he saw as William's vulture-like interest in his lingering decline, while William's agitation about his forthcoming elevation at times seemed so intense that fashionable rakes betted that he would be in a strait-jacket before King George had died.

It was an unprofitable wager. On 26 June 1830 William was woken at six a.m. at Bushy and informed by Sir Henry Halford that George IV was dead and that he was now King of England. Regrettably, one cannot believe the contemporary gossip that he promptly returned to bed remarking that he wished to savour a new experience, 'having never yet slept with a queen'; but there is no doubt that William could not suppress a certain exultation that at last his turn had come. Adelaide was overwhelmed at the prospect of the approaching trial, but William rose enthusiastically to the occasion. Within hours he was whirling in his carriage down the road to Windsor, grinning and bowing to startled bystanders with unregal affability. The reign of William IV had begun.

opposite A contemporary satirical cartoon ridiculing the Duke of Clarence after his resignation as Lord High Admiral.

5 William R

WILLIAM IV ascended the throne at a time when the monarchy was at an almost uniquely low ebb. George IV had set the seal on his unpopularity by combining reckless profligacy and selfish indulgence with a reactionary political viewpoint. In consequence he was regarded with a mixture of loathing and contempt, and his ultimate demise was greeted with callous indifference. 'Nobody was ever less regretted than the late King', Mr Greville noted caustically, while John Cam Hobhouse, expecting emotional demonstrations to mark the King's death, reported in surprise, 'I saw nothing like grief or joy – only a bustle in the streets'. Few people expected that the accession of William would mark the inauguration of a royal revival: speculation still centred mainly on the length of time that would elapse before the new King was formally declared crazy. Yet William's honest geniality and unaffected good humour contrived to ensure that the monarchy was restored to public affection, if not to public veneration. Queen Victoria was to bolster the institution with respect; William provided the goodwill.

The change in atmosphere was apparent almost immediately. George IV had spent his last years skulking in sullen isolation at Windsor, but the new King soon proved refreshingly accessible. 'Hitherto the King has been indefatigable in his efforts to make himself popular, and do good natured and amiable things in every possible instance', Lady Charlotte Williams-Wynn reported to a correspondent in July 1830. 'He opens the communication from Regent Street to the Park, restores the Sunday promenades on the terrace at Windsor, and takes every opportunity of showing himself, driving at a foot's pace through the Park etc. with his head out of the glasses of his carriage the whole way, bowing right and left. This will, of course, after the utter seclusion in which the last two kings have lived come with redoubled effect, and must, at least for a time, render him very popular.' William himself seemed thoroughly to enjoy his new role; Princess Lieven remarked that the saying 'happy as a King' might have been invented with him in mind, and she added that his subjects had become infected by an unwonted animation in their delight at this royal renaissance. 'From grave and depressed they have become possessed of a gaiety, a vivacity, and a movement that makes them scarcely

preceding pages King William IV by Sir William Archer-Shee.

recognizable', she wrote home breathlessly. On occasion William's informality could be carried too far. Shortly after his accession he sauntered out into the London streets for a stroll. Within minutes an excitable crowd had gathered round him, and a whore actually approached him and kissed him on the cheek. The members of White's Club stared aghast at these developments before sallying forth into St James's Street to rescue their sovereign from unwelcome importunities. With some difficulty they escorted him back to the Palace. 'Oh, never mind all this', said William blithely. 'When I have walked about a few times they will get used to it, and will take no notice.' Only stern lectures from Queen Adelaide and the Duke of Wellington sufficed to convince him that such casual amblings were inconsistent with his newly acquired dignity.

Even when performing duties of a formal nature, William seemed incapable of preserving a façade of kingly reserve. At his first Privy Council he greeted its members with an evidently sincere and tolerably graceful eulogy on his departed brother, but he soon reverted to type. 'This is a damned bad pen you have given me', he grumbled audibly as he signed the declaration of his accession. As his Privy Councillors knelt to render him allegiance, he peered at them myopically. 'D'ye know, I am grown so near sighted that I can't make out who you are', he informed the startled Chancellor of the Exchequer. 'You must tell me your name if you please.' His conduct was similarly unrestrained at the late King's funeral. William attended in the capacity of chief mourner, arrayed in a magnificent purple velvet cloak. The solemnity of the occasion failed, however, to impress him. Joseph Jekyll reported that throughout the service he 'talked incessantly and loudly to all about him so that the most frivolous things were overheard', while Lord Ellenborough said of the occasion 'a coronation could hardly be gayer'. After he had endured the service for two hours the King rose from his seat while the anthem was being sung, thanked the Earl Marshal for making the arrangements, and left the church. Yet if William's informal ways sometimes threatened to degenerate into burlesque, on the whole his bluff good nature was welcomed as endearing. *The Times* remarked on 15 July 1830 that William had already 'gained . . . upon the English tastes and prepossessions of his subjects by the blunt and

William's eldest son, George Fitzclarence, Earl of Munster. Even after he had been elevated to the peerage he continued to pester his father for favours and financial endowments.

unaffected – even should it be grotesque – cordiality of his demeanour'.

The King's pleasure in his new prominence was somewhat marred by the deterioration in his relations with his sons. Even William, with his scant conception of propriety, was aware that he could not indiscriminately shower his illegitimate children with honours and promotions without bringing the court into serious disrepute. He therefore proceeded cautiously, appointing his sons to be his equerries and later installing them in higher positions as these became available. George became his Adjutant-General and Adolphus was given the command of the royal yacht. This prudent approach failed to satisfy the

Fitzclarences. In November 1830 his four sons penned him a letter bewailing their fate: 'We are well aware of the cruel position in which we are placed as natural children,' they moaned, 'and feel too acutely that, in the eyes of the law, we are at present nameless and devoid of many rights and advantages of our fellow subjects.' George reminded his father that he had been promised a peerage on two occasions, whilst in India and also before his marriage to Lord Egremont's illegitimate daughter, while his brothers demanded the rank of the younger sons of a Duke. The King, however, felt that he could not confer a peerage on his eldest son until George could afford to live in the style which the dignity of the title demanded. Since William was determined that his limited amount of available money must be shared between all his children, George's ennoblement would inevitably be delayed by this condition. The Fitzclarences' reaction was peremptory: on 26 November they announced their intention to abandon their father's household, and, 'though it reduces us almost to beggary', to resign their appointments. This distressing estrangement was only terminated in May 1831, by which time Lord Egremont had so generously subsidized his son-in-law that William felt that George could sustain the honour of an earldom. George was created Earl Munster, and his brothers and sisters were endowed with the rank of the younger children of a marquis. Even so, the King's relations with his sons were frequently inharmonious. Lord Munster pressed for leave to carry the King's crown at his coronation, a demand so overweening that it provoked even the patient King to complain of his son's 'inordinate ambition and vanity'. While Munster grumbled about his father's disregard of primogeniture, his brothers evinced scant gratitude for their father's efforts on their behalf. Despite William's generosity to him, Frederick Fitzclarence soon embroiled himself in debt and casually sent his father bills totalling £12,000. William said that if he sold his house to liquidate part of the sum, he would make up the difference, an offer which his son did not even deign to acknowledge. Augustus Fitzclarence complained to Fanny Kemble, quite without foundation, that his father had forced him to enter the Church, and abused him in terms so un-christian that Miss Kemble felt obliged to remonstrate. Happily his daughters

Lord Augustus Fitzclarence took Holy Orders after the abandonment of a career at sea, but he claimed, quite unfairly, that he had only become a clergyman because his father had forced him to do so.

113

afforded the King greater satisfaction. Their marriages had ensured that they were painlessly absorbed into society, and their proximity to the King was a source of pleasure rather than humiliation. Their informal presence brightened up the courts, for, as Lady Wharncliffe commented, 'They are all, you know, pretty and lively, and *make society* in a way that real princesses could not.' The King's grandchildren continued to be a rich vein of delight. They were frequently invited to Windsor, where they revelled in being given dancing lessons and being taught to drill in the military style. As a special treat they were permitted to watch the morning ritual in which the King's head was bathed in rosewater.

The King's relations with his brother the Duke of Cumberland were less happy. Cumberland, a sinister, reactionary intriguer, suspected by the public to be capable even of murder, had never been William's favourite brother. 'If the Duke of Cumberland can do mischief or say an ill natured thing he will be sure to do it', he once stoutly assured Lady Bedingfield. Cumberland had exerted an ambiguous influence over George IV, apparently simultaneously repelling and fascinating him. William was determined to be held in no such thraldom. The Duke had persuaded his late brother to appoint him Gold Stick, in command of the household cavalry at Windsor, and had further cajoled him into decreeing that the Gold Stick was directly responsible to the monarch. William crisply vetoed this arrangement, insisting that in future the Gold Stick should be responsible to the Commander-in-Chief. Cumberland huffily resigned. A further disagreement ensued over the stabling arrangements at Windsor: the Duke's horses occupied the Queen's stables and the King sent him a message to remove them. Cumberland growled that he 'would be damned if they should go', but subsequently he was obliged sulkily to comply. Yet there was nothing vindictive in William's treatment of his brother: when the opportunity arose he arranged for him to be given a stately residence at Kew, prompting the Duchess of Cumberland to fall on her knees in gratitude to the King.

The King and Queen divided their time between London, Windsor and Brighton. In London they lived mainly at St James's Palace, although they retained Clarence House. The alterations to Buckingham Palace, an extravaganza commis-

opposite The Duke of Cumberland by G. Dawe. William distrusted the intriguing mind of his reactionary younger brother, and was determined that he should exert little influence at court.

preceding pages: Queen Adelaide and William IV painted by Sir William Archer-Shee.

117

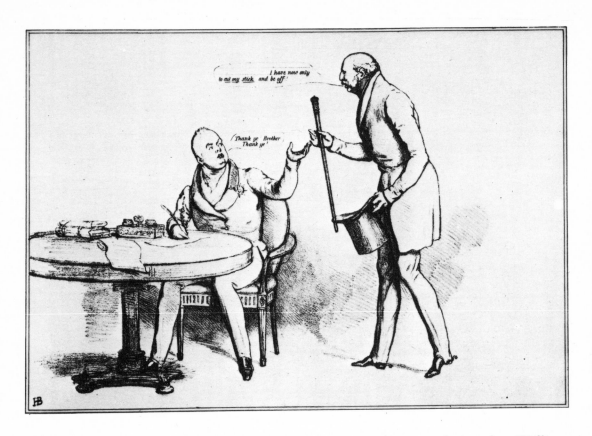

Resignation and Fortitude, a cartoon by John Doyle depicting the King receiving with complete equanimity his brother's resignation as Gold Stick.

sioned by George IV, were nearing completion, but William dreaded the prospect of moving there, testily dismissing the palace as 'a most ill contrived house'. At different times in his reign he suggested that it should be converted into a barracks, or even adopted as the House of Parliament when the old one burnt to the ground in 1834. The ministers firmly resisted these proposals, but in fact William contrived to remain safely lodged at St James's and Queen Victoria was the first sovereign to make Buckingham Palace her domicile. William was not entirely familiar with Windsor on his accession. The day after his brother's funeral he went all over it, seeing some of the rooms for the first time. The novelty soon wore off, however, and he confided that really he would prefer to live at Bushy; but he went to Windsor for the sake of the public. Of the Pavilion at Brighton, on the other hand, he was very fond. One of his grand-daughters later recalled that, when there, he tried 'as far as possible to cast off the trammels of royalty, which always more or less taxed the old King's patience'. Having these

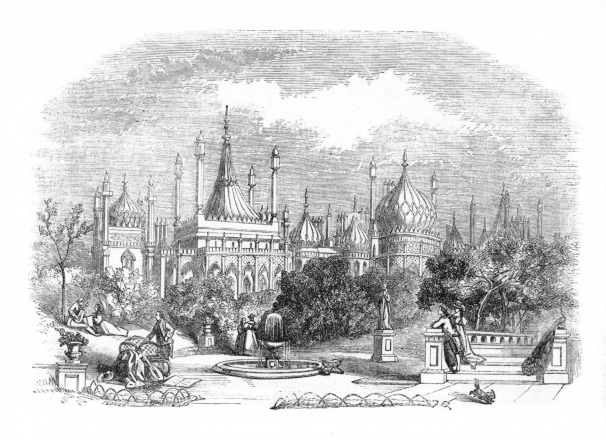

residences at his disposal gave the King ample opportunity to indulge his penchant for entertaining. 'Never was there a king so hospitable', Princess Lieven recorded. Lord Ellenborough noted that the King had about thirty people to dinner every day, and often there were over a hundred. Yet if the King had a naturally generous and outgoing personality, his hospitality was not characterized by lavish extravagance: King George's horde of French chefs was dismissed and homely English ones installed in their place; Lady Williams-Wynn loyally insisted, however, 'Still his dinners are said to be properly handsome'. Others were less appreciative of the new regime: Lord Ravensworth was 'horrified' at the news of the dismissal, while the eccentric Lord Dudley was heard to mutter all too audibly, after dining at the Pavilion, 'What a change, to be sure. Cold pâtés and hot champagne!' At Brighton the King entertained with very little pomp. He would send to the hotels every morning for a list of their guests so that he could invite anyone he knew. 'Come along directly', he would urge his old naval

Brighton Pavilion, where William and Adelaide regularly entertained.

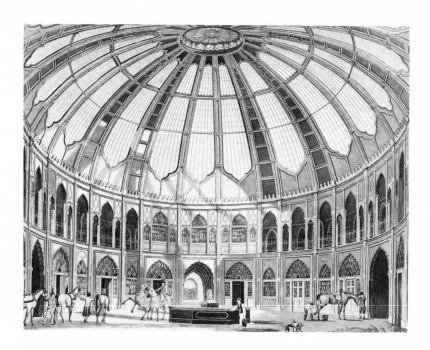

The stables at Brighton Pavilion. Queen Adelaide was a keen horse woman and much enjoyed riding during visits to Brighton.

cronies; 'Do not bother about clothes. The Queen does nothing but embroider flowers after dinner.' Indeed, visitors had to ensure that the King was prevented from slipping from informality into laxity. 'The King was in very good spirits and good fun,' wrote Lady Wharncliffe after a visit to Brighton, 'but one was afraid of *encouraging* him, as he was rather inclined to be *improper* in his jokes.' Queen Adelaide, however, saw that the tone of the court did not degenerate. She forbade ladies to come *decolletées* to her parties, unlike George IV who, liking 'ample expanses of that sort', had practically made them compulsory. The unpretentious nature of the court did not, in the opinion of some sophisticates, compensate for its lack of brilliance. Princess Lieven deplored the lack of informed conversation – 'never a word of politics' – while Lady Grey affirmed after a visit to Windsor that 'all the boring she had ever endured was literally nothing compared with the misery of the two preceding nights'. After dinner the guests habitually sat around a mahogany table while the Queen stitched at her embroidery and the King dozed off, 'occasionally waking for the purpose of saying "Exactly so Ma'am" and then sleeping again'. At large dinners, however, the company was not infrequently enlivened, indeed electrified, by the King's predilection for speechifying, a passion which he could now indulge to the full. Unfortunately William was inclined to become so enthused with his own oratorical powers that his discourses were apt to be not only intolerably verbose, but also decidedly undiplomatic. In the course of one harangue delivered after dinner, he referred to the French King as 'an infamous scoundrel', an indiscretion which earned him a severe rebuke from the Duke of Wellington. It was not long, however, before he was inspired to commit fresh rhetorical excesses. At a dinner for the diplomatic corps William launched into a spontaneous address in French, which he finally concluded by proposing a toast of quite astonishing vulgarity. Nervously, Lord Sefton inquired of Talleyrand, recently appointed French Ambassador in London, what he thought of the performance. '*C'est bien remarquable*', replied the aged diplomat with studied ambigiuty.

Talleyrand, the French statesman and diplomat, who concluded his long career with a spell as French Ambassador to England.

These flourishes of oratory represented the full extent of William's artistic leanings. Paintings failed to interest him. When one of the many works of art purchased by George IV was proudly displayed to him, he commented ingenuously, 'Aye, it seems pretty – I daresay it is – my brother was very fond of this sort of nick nackery.' He indicated that he regarded George's collection as no more than an extravagant fad, and furthermore robustly expressed the view that all paintings of religious objects were improper and ought to be destroyed. He slept soundly through the opera, was suspicious of all writers, and dismissed 'that dry rot, the press' as 'the vehicle of everything that is false and capricious'. As for sport, his attitude was determined more by patriotism than enthusiasm: he found racing tedious but nevertheless kept up the royal stud, albeit somewhat reduced, in the belief that the standard of English bloodstock must be maintained. The fact that William's interests remained those of a parochial country squire was not necessarily unwelcome to his subjects, who shuddered at the memory of the grotesque prodigality perpetrated in the name of culture by George IV. But it was feared that this un-distinguished old gentleman with a head shaped like a pineapple would prove incapable of dealing with those matters of state which were still an inherent part of kingship. In this respect, however, William was agreeably to confound expectations.

Sir Robert Peel, Tory statesman. As the Duke of Wellington's right-hand-man Peel was one of the foremost politicians of the day at the time of William's accession.

opposite Princess Lieven, wife of the Russian Ambassador and an acute observer of political developments and of life at court until her husband's recall to Russia in 1834.

In the first place, he was conscientious in dealing promptly with his duties. Towards the end of his reign George IV had abandoned himself so completely to sloth that he had refused to sign any state papers. William patiently signed the backlog of 48,000 papers that had accumulated during his brother's abdication of responsibility. Every night he laboured through a pile of documents, while Adelaide sat by with a blotter and a bowl of warm water in which he might bathe his painfully cramped fingers. He was aided in his bureaucratic duties by the painstaking and loyal Sir Herbert Taylor. Sir Herbert, a perfect private secretary, never tried to impose his own views on his unpredictable master, but he occasionally sought to soften the impact of some of William's more forthright communications to his ministers with a discreet accompanying note. The King's ministers were suitably impressed at the despatch with which business was conducted. 'If I had been able to deal with my late master as I do with my present I should have got on much better', the Duke of Wellington assured Mr Greville, adding that 'he had done more business with him in ten minutes than with the other in as many days'. William showed an ability to grasp problems intelligently and a determination to master their details. 'Generally speaking he was an excellent man of business,' Lord Brougham claimed, 'unlike his brother, who would ask no questions for fear of showing his ignorance – or his father, who would run on with too many and would not wait for answers. He asked as many as were required to let him fully understand whatever was brought before him and gave his own views with perfect candour and fairness; nor was he the least impatient of contradiction but, on the contrary, rather courted it, in order that he might come to a full understanding with his ministers.' These businesslike qualities were somewhat impaired by a tendency towards somnolence – in one of his first interviews with Peel he slept for twenty minutes out of the half hour granted – but when he was fully alert he showed himself both capable and penetrating.

Yet, while he did not shirk from interesting himself in the affairs of government, nor did he attempt to shape them blindly to his will. He had formulated for himself a constitutional code of conduct in the years immediately before his accession, and already held the convictions on which this code was founded

when his brother accepted his resignation as Lord High Admiral. On that occasion he had written reassuringly to George, 'As the King you could not have done otherwise, *because the King must support his ministers.*' And yet it was not a philosophy to which George IV had subscribed. If political realities prevented him from thwarting his ministers' will whenever it conflicted with his own, this owed nothing to his personal forbearance. Although the monarch could no longer dismiss his Government at will, he could still undermine its position by exhibitions of disloyalty and by indulging in intrigue. To these expedients George IV did not hesitate to resort if his ministers incurred his displeasure. William was determined to eschew such underhand ploys, even believing that he should not take advice from those who were not his ministers. Before his accession William had confided to a friend that when on the throne he intended to 'ban all backstairs influence' in order to promote 'the fullest confidence between the sovereign and his ministers'. Unfortunately, despite William's gallant intentions to abide by these general principles, the exact position of the sovereign in relation to his ministers remained undefined, a situation which would afford opportunity for misunderstandings in the future. William's fundamental code of conduct sometimes proved inadequate to cope with the complexities entailed in balancing the constitutional triangle of King, Lords and Commons, but his adherence to it (punctuated admittedly by occasional deviations of varying gravity) ensured that relations between monarch and minister were free from the poison distilled by suspected bad faith.

When William came to the throne the Duke of Wellington headed a Tory administration. In accordance with his principles, William lost no opportunity to bolster him with almost extravagant demonstrations of loyalty. At his first Council meeting he declared his intentions of giving the ministry 'his entire, determined and cordial support', and when dining with the Duke at Apsley House he reaffirmed this resolve in a rambling speech. After dinner Princess Lieven playfully congratulated the Duke as a man 'whose power to all eternity had been ratified', but in fact William's loyalty to his Tory ministers did not extend to maintaining them in power artificially against the wishes of both Parliament and nation. If the position of the ministers became untenable he would accept their resignations and render the same support to their successors. He hoped, however, that any succeeding administration would be broadly based, composed of moderate men drawn from all parties. For confirmed Whigs he felt a vague distrust: at a Council meeting Lord Bathurst put forward the name of a possible replacement for a county sheriff. 'He is a Whig', William commented ominously. Lord Bathurst assured him that the candidate was nonetheless a worthy choice. 'Oh,' said the King, 'I do not mean to say that it is wrong, only remember, he is a Whig.' Unfortunately William's accession coincided with political developments which made the prospect of a Coalition Government increasingly remote. Affiliation to a party was still by no means an automatic part of political life. Many backbenchers in the unreformed House of Commons owed their seats not to party connections but to local interests, an influential patron, or just straight bribery. Nevertheless, political opinions had crystallized to the extent that differences could not easily be submerged under the cloak of service to the crown. The fairly composite ministry formed by Wellington in January 1828 had already been reduced to an undistinguished, if coherent, Tory rump by the departure of both its left and its right wing. The moderate liberal group headed by Huskisson had seceded from the Government soon after its formation; then in 1829 the Duke had outraged the right wing by his sponsorship of catholic emancipation. They too had deserted him, leaving Wellington presiding over a tottering administration. The Whigs, on the other hand, for years in disarray after an age in opposition, were forming themselves into a viable alternative party throughout 1830. A growing number of MPs now congregated regularly in the Whig Lord Althorp's rooms in Albany, and the party was further strengthened by the accession of a leader of distinction. Lord Grey, a long term proponent of reform, might nevertheless have been tempted to support the Government if Wellington had offered him office. After George IV's death he was provoked by Wellington's neglect of his services into open opposition.

The accession of a monarch necessitated a general election, and, in hopes of strengthening his position by an appeal to the country, Wellington gratefully dissolved Parliament in July.

The Election by Hogarth, 1760. At the time of William's accession, drunkenness, bribery, violence and chaos were as evident at elections as they had been seventy years before. The King himself dreaded elections, which he believed to be periods 'of disorder, of general relaxation and more or less of outrage'.

Protestant Descendancy, a satirical print attacking the Duke of Wellington for his support of the Bill for Catholic Emancipation, passed in April 1829. His action not only enraged the right-wing of the Tory party but ran contrary to public opinion, and the Duke's support of emancipation was to contribute to the growing weakness of his administration.

Yet the results were unhelpful: owing to the perversions in the electoral system it seemed that the Government could still command a majority in the Commons, but in those constituencies where any semblance of free political opinion prevailed the trend in public feeling seemed unmistakable. On studying the returns, Mr Greville pronounced 'The signs of the times are all for reform and retrenchment', while Lord Grey felt he could count on an increase of fifty votes in a division. Then, in early August, news arrived of a revolution in France, toppling Charles X from his throne in favour of the citizen King, Louis Philippe. The intelligence came too late to effect the outcome of the elections substantially, but throughout the autumn it nevertheless contributed to an atmosphere pregnant with expectation. The situation was further exacerbated by the widespread distress of the agricultural labourers. The last two harvests had been bad, and the prospect of another cruel winter must have seemed almost unendurable to the rural poor. Throughout the autumn of 1830 a wave of violent disturbances

swept the country districts. Threshing machines were wrecked, hayricks burned. In these circumstances firm governance was necessary, leadership of a kind that Wellington's ministry seemed unable to provide. Furthermore, and perhaps of greater significance, the general distress helped sharpen discontent with the imperfections in the constitutional system.

That system was characterized by anachronism and anomaly. In 1830 the constitution remained effectively the same as that operative when George III ascended the throne, and had indeed not changed in substance since the union with Scotland. In 1760 the population of England, Wales and Scotland stood at a mere eight million; by 1830 it had grown to about sixteen and a half million. There had been no corresponding increase in the size of the electorate. Furthermore, the electoral system took no cognizance of developments resulting from the vast strides of industrialization in the previous fifty years. Much of the surplus population had been absorbed into new urban centres, to fuel the labour demands of new factories. Yet the distribution of

In the autumn of 1830 economic distress in rural districts precipitated a frightening wave of revolts directed against farmers and landowners. Haystacks were burnt, and threshing machines, which were believed to deprive the labourers of employment in the winter months, were another popular target for destruction.

parliamentary seats quite disregarded regional alterations in the population structure: places which had long since faded into insignificance continued to return two members to Westminster, while the teeming masses of the burgeoning industrial towns had no one to champion their rights. Birmingham, Manchester and Leeds, numbering a total of 500,000 inhabitants by 1830, did not return a single member to the elective assembly; conversely in the county of Cornwall there were forty-four parliamentary seats. The particularly notorious case of Old Sarum had turned that borough into something of a tourist attraction: visitors flocked to see the ruined castle and ancient earthworks that returned two members to the legislature. Even in the more populous boroughs the number of actual voters could be ludicrously small. The rules governing the franchise qualification varied from borough to borough, but, while in a few cases the right to vote was quite widely distributed, in others it was confined to a tiny proportion of the inhabitants. A handful of voters could easily be controlled by a rich or influential man, and in many cases the election represented little more than a formality, the electors obediently registering their support for the candidate nominated by their patron. Some seats came to be regarded as a piece of disposable property, good prices being paid on the open market for a constituency which guaranteed a place in the House of Commons. Mr Croker, a contemporary political commentator, estimated that 276 seats were controlled by individuals, and of these 203 were Tories. Even in parliamentary boroughs with a large electorate, or in the county seats where the suffrage was wider, the absence of any sort of secret ballot meant that the outcome of contests could be determined by the exertion of local pressure and bribery on a large scale. Only when a massive surge of public opinion in favour of the Whigs enabled independent opinion to prevail against these inducements could that party hope for a working majority in the Commons.

Parliamentary reform had been a political issue for over fifty years, although originally the question had revolved around the demand to adjust the imbalance in the constitution which assured the crown's unacceptable predominance. This grievance had eventually been remedied by administrative rather than political reform and, with this redress, respectable

above How to get made an MP, a satirical cartoon of July 1830, attacking the venal political system of the day. A prospective parliamentary candidate is handing a substantial cash sum to a patron who controls the voters in an electoral borough, and who guarantees to him that his return is now assured.

well here's the Cash. as for the Votes leave them to you

right George Canning painted by Sir Thomas Lawrence. Canning's professed opposition to any measure of parliamentary reform had helped to ensure that it was not a prominent issue throughout the 1820s. However, his death in 1827 facilitated its re-emergence in the forefront of politics.

support for constitutional reform wavered. The trend was sharply accelerated by the excesses of the French Revolution, which converted all but radicals or visionaries into convinced opponents of change. Even when the reverberations of that great convulsion began to fade in the 1820s, the policies of judicious innovation pursued by Lord Liverpool's Government did not extend to embracing parliamentary reform, while

Canning's opposition to any such measure further condemned it to obscurity. By 1830, however, circumstances combined to bring reform once again into the forefront of politics. The question of catholic emancipation had dominated domestic issues since the union with Ireland. That contentious question had now been dealt with, incidentally leaving its implacable opponents demanding that any Parliament capable of passing such an act in defiance of public opinion should be purged by reform. Other domestic issues assumed secondary importance to parliamentary reform, which was felt to be an essential preliminary to the achievement of fresh objectives. Thus Thomas Attwood, a passionate proponent of currency reform, founded the Birmingham Political Union in January 1830, in the belief that successful agitation for parliamentary reform would secure a House of Commons more amenable to changes in financial policy. Moreover, recent revelations of gross electoral corruption had served to highlight the failures of the system, while the Government's decision to prosecute several newspapers had encouraged the suggestion that a corrupt and unrepresentative administration was bridling free expression. Against these currents of protest were stacked the arguments of the traditionalists. The very eccentricity of the constitution, they argued, guaranteed its inimitable balance; any tampering would irrevocably wreck the delicate machinery. The domination of elections by a small clique of patrons did no more than preserve deference and stability. Adjustments would lead to the disappearance of these blessings and pave the way to anarchy.

Nevertheless, sensible men attuned to public feeling acknowledged that some concession over parliamentary reform would be necessary in the not too distant future. The more cautious hoped it would be a minor measure to act as a sop to reform agitation. 'What they all feel . . .' said Greville, 'is that by a timely concession and regulating the present spirit real improvements might be made and extreme measures avoided.' The Duke of Wellington, however, was not prepared to compromise his principles for the sake of political expediency. His administration showed every intention of pursuing a firmly orthodox course. The King's speech composed for the opening of Parliament in November 1830 was authoritarian in tone. Worse was to follow: in reply to a speech by Lord Grey

above A cartoon by John Doyle, showing William receiving his new Prime Minister, Lord Grey, for the first time, while in the background the Duke of Wellington gets his marching orders from John Bull. The King is shown readily agreeing to Grey's proposals for 'peace, retrenchment and reform', although in reality he viewed the policies of the new Whig Government with considerable apprehension.

right A cartoon depicting the dejected Wellington and Peel after their resignations had been accepted by the King.

132

containing a cautious reference to parliamentary reform, Wellington rose to speak of a largely discredited constitutional system in terms of extravagant eulogy. 'I am fully convinced that the country possesses at the present moment a legislature which answers all the good purposes of legislation,' he rhapsodized in the course of this address, 'and this to a greater degree than any legislature ever has answered in any country whatever'. He sat down amidst stunned silence. 'I have not said too much have I?' he enquired of the Foreign Secretary, Aberdeen. 'You'll hear of it' came the grim reply.

He did. Government funds promptly fell three per cent and London abounded with rumours that a wave of insurrection was about to sweep away the established order. On 9 November the King was due to dine with his ministers at the Guildhall. Reports filtered to the Government that the occasion would be marked by murderous riots. Alderman Key warned the ministers he could not guarantee their safety. Painfully unnerved by these communications, the Government decided to cancel the dinner. The King appeared to accept the decision in good grace and continued to treat his advisers with cordiality, but his faith in their capacities was crumbling. It began to look increasingly likely that the administration could not survive the approaching division on the motion of parliamentary reform tabled by the demonic member for Yorkshire, Henry Brougham, at the beginning of the session. In the event they were spared the trial: on 15 November the disparate groups in the opposition united to beat the Government by a majority of twenty-nine in a debate on the civil list. The next morning Wellington resigned.

The King was upset at this development, but resolved not to interfere. When the ministers came for their farewell interview Mr Greville reported that 'he received them with great kindness, shed tears, but accepted their resignation without remonstrance'. The outgoing ministers performed a last service to their master: all of them, except for the Duke, assured the King of the necessity for some measure of reform. The thought was not appealing to the King. He viewed the prospect of change with suspicion and alarm. Nevertheless, he believed he must submerge his own prejudices in deference to his ministers' advice. William's political honeymoon was over.

133

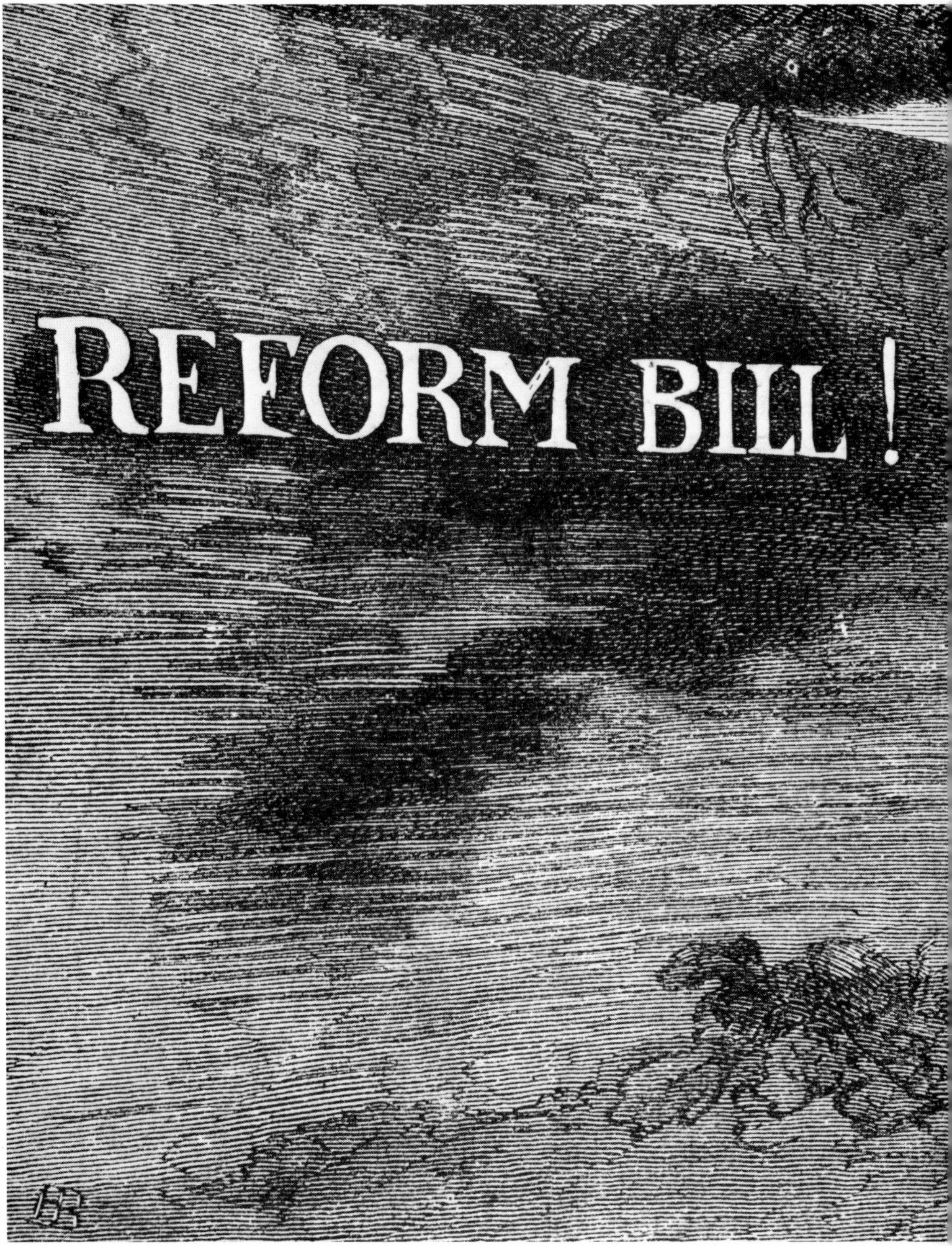
REFORM BILL !

6 The Two Bills

W HEN WELLINGTON HAD TAKEN his leave of the King, William had apprehensively enquired what he knew of the leader of the Whigs, Lord Grey. The Duke had curtly replied that he 'really did not know, but that he had the reputation of being an ill-tempered violent man'. This impression was misleading: William was to find Lord Grey far from wild. Of the most aristocratic bearing, and one of the most distinguished orators of his day, Grey often evinced almost as much distaste for the strong measures he felt constrained to adopt in the course of the Reform Bill crisis as did William himself. His belief in the necessity for reform was, however, of long standing, and at his first interview with the King, Grey made it clear that he could only accept the premiership on condition that he could bring in a measure of reform. To this William agreed. Grey's Cabinet was quite broadly based. Several moderate liberals accepted office, Palmerston being given the Foreign Office and Melbourne appointed Home Secretary, while a Tory reformer, the Duke of Richmond, became Postmaster General. Of the old Whigs, Althorp was made leader of the House of Commons and Chancellor of the Exchequer and Durham became Lord Privy Seal. One problem remained: Henry Brougham, the unpredictable, if brilliant, member for Yorkshire must somehow be absorbed in the administration, for the Government could not hope to survive the session if confronted with his formidable opposition in the Commons. Brougham indicated that he would find the offer of the Mastership of the Rolls very acceptable, but the King, who had been warned by Wellington not to permit Brougham to attain too dominant a position within the ministry, refused to sanction the appointment. Brougham's only response to the ministers' next offer of the Attorney-Generalship was to tear up the letter bearing the invitation and stamp on the pieces. Reluctantly, however, he agreed to become Lord Chancellor, despite his knowledge that he would be unable to dominate the House of Lords as he did the lower chamber. The King was delighted at the satisfactory outcome to these negotiations, reserving the credit largely to himself. To Lord Holland he asserted conspiratorially, 'You are all under great obligations to me. I have settled Brougham. He will not be dangerous any more.'

The King showed himself anxious to be civil towards his new

preceding pages As fervour for reform increased throughout the country, walls were plastered with slogans in support of the Bill. In this good-natured cartoon John Doyle pokes gentle fun at the King, who is represented peering at one such slogan and wondering 'Can that mean me?'

ministers. When Brougham apologetically produced a pile of petitions for the King's attention from a great bag, William breezily signified that he 'would willingly receive anything from that bag except the seals'. Lord Grey was hospitably welcomed at Brighton in December, when even the Queen, who felt acute alarm at the prospect of a reforming ministry, exuded so much goodwill that Grey informed Princess Lieven that he had 'quite fallen in love' with Her Majesty. These cordial relations were facilitated by the fact that William approved of the vigorous measures adopted by Melbourne at the Home Office to stamp out the disturbances in the southern counties which had characterized the autumn of 1830. Melbourne's instructions to the magistrates resulted in the execution of three offenders and the transportation of between four and five hundred others to Australia. William was not an inhumane man but he heartily applauded such policies. This was not surprising. Incomprehension of the economic forces that had driven the labourers to revolt precluded compassion for their cause from respectable quarters. If Melbourne, for all his cynical intelligence and indolent good humour, could be moved to denounce the rioters as motivated by 'the most pure, and unmixed, and diabolical feelings of senseless malignity', it was hardly likely that William's understanding should extend further.

The policy of the ministry was, however, two-pronged, combining domestic repression with political concession. Soon after the formation of the Government a committee of four, headed by Durham, was formed to draw up a draft Reform Bill. Its instructions were to devise a measure which would so satisfy public opinion that demands for further reform would be stifled, while preserving the essential characteristics of the constitution. If William had been prevailed upon to accept that the question of reform must be tackled, he had not supported the cause with any pleasure, and as the committee of four pored over their calculations, his trepidation increased. He could not refrain from tentative suggestions that public feelings on reform were 'overrated by those who were . . . strenuous advocates of reform', and that the introduction of a measure might profitably be delayed until the times were more propitious. These doubts were little more than expressions of wishful thinking on

right A drawing from the sketchbook of Lady Caroline Lamb of her husband, the urbane and charming Lord Melbourne, who became Home Secretary in Lord Grey's Government. He proceeded against those who had participated in the revolts in the rural south with the utmost severity.

opposite The King's private secretary, Sir Herbert Taylor. Loyal and diligent, Sir Herbert often formed the channel of communication between the King and his ministers.

the part of William, and when Grey insisted that to delay reform would be to court disaster he promptly conceded the point. Grey, however, interpreted the King's waverings as an ominous confirmation of his suspicions that William was surrounded by a reactionary Tory *camarilla* who persistently strove to erode the King's attachment to his ministers. These worries, which tormented Grey throughout the whole reform crisis, were on the whole greatly exaggerated. It is true that the majority of those who constituted the King's most intimate society were distinctly right wing in their thinking. Furthermore, almost all the royal family, including the Fitzclarences, were against reform, while the Queen's political philosophy bore the rather primitive imprint of her upbringing in benevolently despotic Saxe-Meiningen. Nevertheless, as Sir Herbert Taylor repeatedly assured Lord Grey, the King

scrupulously refrained from political consultations with anyone but his ministers. In general the Queen voluntarily resisted the temptation to interfere with political affairs. She told Miss Clitherow, an old friend and a regular visitor to Windsor, 'I must have my own opinion, but I do not talk to the King about it. It would only make him unhappy and do no good.' Even when she transgressed this admirable rule and on one occasion expressed a controversial view, the King merely roared at her, 'Madam, English politics are not to be understood by any German'. But it is difficult to be sure that in private he was always so unresponsive. In the bedroom the prejudices of the Queen might have commanded more attention. The fact that the King conscientiously strove to avoid being contaminated by the principles of his entourage could not necessarily prevent their collective viewpoints from having an insidious effect on his loyalties. Grey's worries were exaggerated but not entirely groundless.

On 30 January 1831, Grey journeyed nervously to Brighton to lay in front of the King the plan of reform approved by the Cabinet. He found William in an alert and amenable frame of mind. On the following day he wrote to Brougham with undisguised relief: 'The King entered into every part of the reform with great care, and, I must add, with great acuteness, and in the end understood it completely. The result is that it has his full and entire approbation.'

On 4 February the King wrote to Grey to elaborate his views on the proposed scheme. He made it clear that his attitude to reform was far from enthusiastic. Indeed, had the measure submitted to him proposed the introduction of election by ballot, or even worse, universal suffrage, he would have withheld his consent altogether. Furthermore, he already perceived, and dreaded, the possibility that the House of Lords might reject a Reform Bill already passed by the Commons, thereby provoking 'a quarrel between these two branches of the legislature . . . upon a popular question . . . to be viewed as a great national and political calamity'. But he concluded this alarming disquisition with a firm avowal of support for his ministers' proposals, averring that 'serious as were his apprehensions and objections, they have been removed by the nature and character of the proposed measure'. He trusted his support

Lord John Russell, who, although not in the Cabinet, was a member of the committee of four which drafted the Reform Bill.

would be all the more valuable in view of the fact that it had not been given lightly.

The exact provisions of the Reform Bill remained a closely guarded secret between the King and his chief ministers. Only on 1 March 1831 did Lord Russell, 'a little fellow not weighing above eight stone', rise to unfold to the Commons the details of one of the most momentous pieces of legislation ever set before the House. He opened with a tedious review of constitutional history dating back to medieval times, but his yawning audience were jolted into rapt attention when he embarked on the detailed outline of the Bill's clauses. Sixty English rotten boroughs were to lose both members; a further forty-seven were to lose one each, the seats being redistributed among the more populous counties and unrepresented boroughs with more than 10,000 inhabitants. The borough franchise was

141

Lord John Russell
introducing the Reform
Bill in the Commons. The
proposals contained in the
Bill had been kept a closely
guarded secret, and when
Russell, 'a little fellow not
weighing above eight
stone', revealed the extent
of its provisions in March
1831 both sides of the
House were stunned.

uniformly extended to occupiers of houses worth at least £10 a year. Few of his audience had anticipated anything approaching so sweeping a measure; as Russell continued with his inexorable catalogue of seats earmarked for disfranchisement, the Tories greeted each announcement with wild ironical laughter. Even some Whigs, stupefied by the extent of the measure fostered by their leaders, were heard to exclaim, 'They're mad! They're mad!' Yet the Government had decided that any measure less formidable in scope would act as a mere palliative, and could not prevent potentially dangerous agitation for further reform. That the King had submitted to so extensive a Bill in deference to these arguments was remarkable. Whether Parliament would prove equally visionary remained to be seen.

Had Peel called for an immediate division when Russell sat down the Bill might have been thrown out at once. Instead he abided by his party's original plan to debate the proposals thoroughly before dividing on the second reading, believing that a merciless analysis of the Bill's inequities would turn many members from supporting it. Yet the delay ensured that details of the Bill became common knowledge, and the pressure of popular enthusiasm could be potently persuasive in converting wavering backbenchers in favour of it. Nevertheless, the outcome of the debate remained uncertain. Lord Grey, hitherto sanguine about the passage of the Bill through the Commons, panicked when the opposition united on 18 March to defeat the Government on the Timber Duty Bill. If his opponents could muster such strength on such a minor issue, he began to doubt whether the House of Commons as present constituted would ever pass so contentious a measure as reform.

Nervously, Grey asked Sir Herbert Taylor if he thought the King would consider dissolving Parliament if the Commons rejected the Bill. An election could then be fought with reform as the principal issue. Sir Herbert passed this communication to the King, whose reaction was uncompromising. An election campaign centring on so inflammable a platform would convulse the entire country, and Ireland in particular would be engulfed in revolution. He could not contemplate authorizing dissolution in such inauspicious circumstances. Grey's distress at this confidential communication was increased when details of its gist appeared in the newspapers. Whether the information emanated from the royal household he could only speculate, but he felt that uncommitted members would be more likely to oppose the Bill if they felt assured that they would not have to confront their angry constituents in the near future. He viewed the division on the second reading with increasing trepidation. The House divided on 23 March 1831. Large sums of money were wagered on the outcome, and tension mounted as it became apparent that the vote would be very close. Finally the tellers announced the figures: the second reading had been passed by 302 votes to 301. The reaction of the reformers was ecstatic: 'We burst into tumults of delight, clapping hands, waving hats and shouting lustily', John Cam Hobhouse later recalled. The King, too, expressed his delight at the outcome, and gave the Government a practical demonstration of solidarity by dismissing from his household three officers who had voted against the Bill.

But this was only a temporary reprieve. The opposition were far from cowed and evinced a firm determination to dismember the Bill in committee. Lord Grey conveyed to the King that if an amendment inimical to the fundamental principles of the Bill was carried he would again request permission for a dissolution. The King apparently remained firmly obdurate: he claimed that reports on the state of Ireland had only confirmed his resistance. The prospects of the Government surviving seemed increasingly slim. On 20 April 1831 General Gascoyne's amendment that the number of seats in England and Wales should not be reduced was passed by a majority of eight votes. The Government elected to regard this as a question of fundamental significance, and informed the King that he must either grant a dissolution or accept their resignations. They received his reply the next day. To their surprise he wrote that, while he still felt the full force of his objections to dissolution, the dangers of a second change of administration within such a short space of time led him to concede to his ministers' request as 'the lesser of two evils'. In all probability the King had been bluffing his ministers when he insisted that he would never consent to dissolution, hoping that they would be more disposed to accept amendments to the Bill if they believed the alternative was resignation, but secretly believing the formation of any other ministry unfeasible. The Whigs, however, showed

The King's first cousin William Frederick, Duke of Gloucester. Many people are under the impression that William IV was known to his contemporaries as 'Silly Billy', but in fact this nickname belonged to his cousin.

no resentment at William's guile. 'The King is a good King, the best we ever had', proclaimed Mr Hobhouse in delight.

For the Tories, however, it was a less agreeable surprise, and the shock left them angry and embittered. 'Who is Silly Billy now?' spat William's cousin the Duke of Gloucester, himself usually favoured with this nickname. They determined to be as obstructive as possible before Parliament was dismissed. On the evening of 21 April Lord Wharncliffe announced that the following day he would move an address to the crown against dissolution. Alarmed at the effect this might have on public opinion, Grey and Brougham hastened to the King on the morning of 22 April and begged him to forestall Wharncliffe by proceeding to Parliament immediately and dissolving it in person. Despite his initial aversion to a dissolution, William resented what he regarded as an unwarrantable interference with his prerogative, and proved energetically willing to co-operate. When Lord Grey apologized that the proceedings were so unexpectedly rushed, the King genially riposted, 'Never mind that, I am always at single anchor'. In his enthusiasm, he hardly questioned that Brougham had already ordered an escort of Horse Guards to be in readiness in anticipation of his consent. The necessary arrangements were frenziedly set in motion. The Master of the Horse, Lord Albemarle, was summoned from his breakfast table with an urgent command that the state coach must be hastily prepared. He hurried to the Palace to explain that some delay was inevitable: the manes of the cream-coloured horses that drew the carriage would have to be plaited. 'Then I will go in a hackney coach', the King returned excitably. Despite Albemarle's dithering, the coach arrived in time and William rattled off towards the House of Lords.

In that august assembly the proceedings had meanwhile deteriorated into riotous farce. Against the background of the booming gun salutes that heralded the King's approach, Lord Wharncliffe was endeavouring to move his address. The Duke of Richmond sought to obstruct him by raising points of order, valiantly ignoring Lord Lyndhurst's shaking fist on the other side of the House. Lord Londonderry was flourishing his whip at Richmond and roaring abuse, struggling to free himself from the five peers who clung to his coat-tails in a bid to restrain him

147

from further violence. The scene, in Hansard's guarded phrase, was characterized by 'altogether immense confusion'.

The uproar penetrated to the robing room where the King was preparing himself for the ceremony. Puzzled, he asked Brougham for an explanation. 'If it please Your Majesty, it is the Lords debating', the Chancellor replied adroitly. Undaunted, the King demanded his regalia, set his crown upon his head, and stumped into the chamber. The hubbub dwindled at the entry of the King. William seated himself on the throne and, crown awry, glared angrily around. He proceeded to declare the Parliament prorogued with a view to its immediate dissolution. An unmistakable note of triumph was detectable in his voice.

Yet this exultation was the product of purely transitory excitement. Even as he returned in the coach to the Palace, his depression at the prospect of the future renewed. The cheering crowds which thronged his route home in the belief that his actions had stemmed from personal zeal for reform, were hardly congenial to one who had consented to dissolution 'as the lesser of two evils'. He was particularly displeased when the ministers failed to prevent many public buildings – even the Admiralty – being illuminated in celebration of the dissolution. Predictably the mob in the streets became unruly, and soon were gleefully stoning Tory strongholds such as Apsley House, whose windows remained defiantly sombre. Worse still, the Queen was obliged to return that night through the thronged streets after a visit to a concert. Angered at her known hostility to reform, the crowd surged menacingly around her coach and her footmen were obliged to beat off the press with their canes to prevent individuals thrusting their faces through the windows. The King was infuriated that his wife had been subjected to so distressing an experience. Having welcomed her safely home, he grumpily declared that in view of his ministers' irresponsibility they should not have the privilege of his company at a forthcoming civic dinner at the Guildhall.

Increasingly, the King was preoccupied with the knowledge that the dissolution had brought the prospect of a clash between Lords and Commons appreciably closer. It was anticipated that the election would result in a considerable majority for the reformers, but even if the Bill sailed through the Commons on

opposite Earl Grey, Prime Minister at the time of the Reform Bill. Although prepared to accept extreme measures in order to secure the passage of the Reform Bill, the aristocratic Lord Grey was distressed by the necessity of forcing these upon the King. During the Reform Bill crisis William came to respect and trust him.

Parliament's reassembly there was every probability that the Peers would retain an unremitting hostility to the measure. With this grim thought in mind, William directed another extensive memorandum to Lord Grey two days after the dissolution. He pleaded with him to modify the Bill, thus making it palatable to the more moderate of its noble opponents. Grey's response was a courteous negative. In his opinion it would be necessary to mangle the Bill so horribly to render it acceptable to the Lords that he would be unable to induce a majority in the House of Commons to vote for it. Public feeling demanded 'the Bill, the whole Bill and nothing but the Bill', and to this pressure the Lords must be made to bow.

To the King's distress, the elections emphatically confirmed Lord Grey's estimate of public opinion. 'The King is as frightened as an idiot can be', wrote the Tory Mr Arbuthnot bitterly as the possibility of compromise receded in the face of the overwhelming success of reform candidates at the polls. Feelings ran so high that elections were successfully contested in places where a patron's candidate had previously been returned without demur. The Tory Duke of Northumberland did not even dare run a candidate in his own county, while Lord Worcester only narrowly escaped drowning at the hands of an enraged mob in the course of his campaign. The fact that his own name was invoked to whip up support for reforming candidates – 'Vote for the two Bills' being a popular formula – was scant consolation to the King. To Grey he displayed an unwonted cynicism in assessing the value of the expressions of personal allegiance which had been a feature of the campaign. 'He cannot help subscribing these effusions of loyalty to the gratification of popular clamour by his sanction of a popular measure rather than to any feeling upon which such reliance could be placed', wrote the King with chilling scorn.

Despite the results of the elections, William continued to implore his ministers to modify the Bill. They obstinately refused. Nevertheless, he persisted in supporting them loyally, even investing Lord Grey with the garter in May 1831, despite there being no vacancy in the order. In June Parliament reassembled and the Bill was reintroduced into the Commons. On 7 July it passed its second reading by 367 votes to 231. The

Tories, however, were far from abject in defeat. As the Bill entered the committee stage they continued to display a surprising capacity for ferocious aggression. Every clause of the Bill was bitterly debated, Sir Charles Wetherell and Mr Croker pouring withering scorn on the Government benches. Ostensibly these attacks were to little purpose, for the Tories only succeeded in pushing through one amendment of such slight significance that the Government was prepared to absorb it into the Bill. But their tactics were sound. The prolonged committee proceedings had delayed the Bill being sent to the Lords, providing an interval in which the public excitement on reform might subside and enabling their Lordships to consolidate their ranks in opposition. For William it was a distressing summer. If the Bill could occasion such bitterness in the Commons, what was to be expected when it was submitted to the Lords?

It was perhaps as well that his mind was diverted throughout these months by the consideration of his approaching coronation. It was not, admittedly, a distraction which the King found very soothing. To a man of his earthy common sense the elaborate ceremonial of the coronation consisted of little more than empty pomp, laced with a suspect dash of mysticism. To Grey he grumbled that the ceremony entailed 'useless and ill-timed expense' and would encourage 'popular effervescence', and that a simple service whereby he took the prescribed oath before the assembled Lords and Commons could profitably be substituted for it. But his subjects were not to be cheated of the full majestic ritual, the Tories being particularly insistent that traditions must be maintained. Grudgingly William resigned himself to the ordeal, although specifying that the proceedings should be 'short and cheap'. This condition was fulfilled as far as possible. The eventual cost of his coronation, which occurred on 8 September, was only a little over £30,000, in comparison with £240,000 squandered on that of George IV. Unnecessary extravagances, such as an outlay on a commemorative feast, were dispensed with altogether. Opinions about William's deportment at the ceremony differed: Lady Wharncliffe reported that the King did better than she expected, despite a certain infirmity in his step. But Macaulay was less charitable: 'The bearing of the King made the foolish parts of the

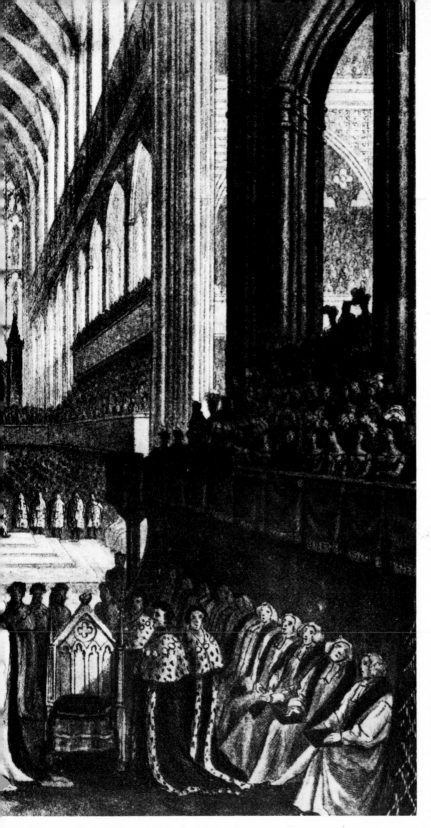

William IV's coronation. William had hoped to dispense with an elaborate ceremony but he was persuaded to endure the full ordeal, and even had to submit to being kissed by the Bishops. He specified, however, that the proceedings should be as 'short and cheap' as possible.

ceremony appear very ridiculous', he grumbled, although even he admitted that the moment of crowning was 'very fine'. Despite the criticisms, the coronation was agreed to have been a success: 'Whereas nobody was satisfied before it, everybody was after it', Mr Greville summarized the proceedings.

Nevertheless, the goodwill it generated was insufficient to defuse the passions distilled by reform. On 22 September 1831 the Bill passed its final reading in the House of Commons and was sent up to the Lords. A formidable debate ensued, marked by a particularly memorable speech from Brougham, who, fortified by constant draughts of mulled port, subjected their Lordships to an impassioned appeal on behalf of reform. He concluded on his bended knees, a theatrical excess which his enemies unkindly attributed to a surfeit of alcohol. The Lords remained unmoved. In the early hours of 8 October 1831 they rejected the Bill by 199 votes to 158, a majority of forty-one.

The King heard the news with a certain melancholy satisfaction. 'His Majesty would deceive Earl Grey if he were to say the result is not such as he had long expected; that even the majority is not larger than he had expected', he wrote with a touch of smugness on receiving the figures for the division. 'It would be idle . . . to admit now he had not anticipated such a result, if the Bill should be carried to the House of Lords without such essential modifications as should render it more palatable to its opponents.' Nevertheless, while he felt that his own assessment of the situation had been proved emphatically correct, he was far from rejoicing at his ministers' discomfiture. He urged them to stay in office and introduce another Bill, which, although preserving the fundamentals of the original, would nevertheless incorporate some concessions to the more moderate of their opponents. He made it clear, however, that their only alternative would be resignation, for he would not contemplate consenting to measures 'which no government could propose and no sovereign consent to', namely, a creation of peers on a scale that would secure an artificial majority for reform in the upper house. At the time, indeed, Lord Grey himself concurred that a creation on such a scale was 'out of the question'. He agreed that the Government should introduce a fresh Bill which, although 'not . . . less efficient' than the original, would possibly contain some alterations. Accordingly

Parliament was prorogued in order that a new Bill might be drawn up.

The intermission was to afford the King scant repose. Tension at court was heightened by the dismissal of the Queen's Chamberlain, Lord Howe. A fawning sycophant upon whom the Queen doted to such an extent that the more imaginatively prurient of her subjects assumed they must be lovers, Howe was a virulent opponent of reform. He had already been warned in May 1831 that his opposition should be conducted in such a way as not to compromise the Queen and King, but had taken little notice. When he voted with the majority in the Lords in October, Grey induced the King to pressure Howe into resignation. The Queen was incensed at what she saw as a secret conspiracy to deprive her of a valued friend, and made no attempt to hide her displeasure. Nor did she confine herself to ostentatious sulking: in her correspondence with Howe she came very close to political intrigue, giving him confidential details of the King's state of mind. 'He sees everything in the right light', she was to inform Howe in January 1832, 'but I am afraid has the fixed idea that no other administration could be formed at present among your friends . . . I should like to know what the Duke of Wellington thinks.' Howe promptly passed the communication on to Wellington.

Harassed by unfortunate domestic upheavals, the King could find little comfort in the political situation. Hopes that a Reform Bill acceptable to both the Government and the Lords could be constructed now seemed over sanguine. Negotiations had been instituted with Lords Wharncliffe and Harrowby, leaders of the 'Waverers', a moderate group of peers who accepted the necessity of some degree of reform. But increasingly Grey felt it unlikely that he would be able to alter the Bill to their specifications: to do so would fatally emasculate it. Furthermore, neither Wharncliffe nor Harrowby seemed influential enough to guarantee to Grey that they could persuade a majority in the Lords to accept even an altered Bill, and he could see little point in making sweeping concessions on a purely speculative basis.

The situation was alarmingly complicated by the wave of violent protest that had greeted the Lords' rejection of the Bill. There were riots in Derby and Nottingham, where the castle

Following the rejection of the Reform Bill by the House of Lords, England was beset by a wave of revolt. In Nottingham the castle, property of the reactionary Duke of Newcastle, was burnt to the ground.

was razed to the ground. Then, in late October, Bristol was gripped by an orgy of riot and plunder, resulting in maybe as many as 400 casualties before peace was restored. Against this background of civil disorder it seemed possible that the Political Unions, associations initially formed to agitate peaceably for reform, might become more militant. They threatened to arm themselves, ostensibly to assist in the maintenance of the peace, but the Government was well aware that its weapons could be turned against the established order. The King deplored the proceedings of the Political Unions, which he indignantly described as 'palpably illegal and treasonable', but he showed no disposition to panic. When the Duke of Wellington sent the King an alarmist report that the Birmingham Political Union had contracted for a large quantity of arms, he assured Lord Grey that he had found the communication 'unnecessary'. Nevertheless, it was clear that the Government must act to prevent the situation from escalating. Yet they dared not

embark on restrictive measures while the public were excited by the belief that the action of the Lords could deprive them of reform. Only the announcement that Parliament would re-assemble in the immediate future and that a new Bill would be introduced as quickly as possible would reassure the people that the Government did not intend to capitulate to their enemies and abandon serious reform. On 21 November they therefore declared that Parliament should reassemble on 6 December. On the following day they issued a proclamation banning the militarized Political Unions. The imminent assembly of Parliament and the necessity of drawing up a new Bill prevented the negotiations with the Waverers being constructively pro-longed, and on 29 November they were finally terminated. They had not been entirely futile: although the Government had been unable to meet the Waverers' main demands, they were able to incorporate some minor points into the new Bill which they trusted would render it less offensive to the Upper

In late October 1831 the visit to Bristol by Sir Charles Wetherell, the unpopular recorder of the city and a virulent opponent of reform, sparked off three days of riot and plunder, possibly resulting in as many as four hundred casualties.

House. But it was an inescapable fact that the attempt at compromise had broken down. It was now very probable that strong executive action would be required to secure the passage of the Bill.

To one of the King's formidable common sense it seemed incomprehensible that the Lords could permit matters to have reached this stage. He observed to Brougham in exasperation 'that *he* was quite clear the shock of the change was over-rated, and that, when once the Bill was passed, things would slide into an easy and quiet posture as before'; why then did the Tories persist in clinging to their exaggerated fears? By their intransigent opposition they had manoeuvred him into a position where he would find it difficult to withhold his consent to measures which he believed to be of infinitely greater violence than reform. He made his views clear to the Archbishop of Canterbury, in the desperate hope that the latter would pass them on to the episcopal bench in the Lords and induce the prelates to support reform.

It became increasingly dubious that such expedients would be sufficient to secure the Bill a majority in the Lords. More and more, discussion in the Cabinet was revolving around the question of a creation of peers. By late December Grey was hinting to the King that the matter would have to be considered. At a Cabinet Meeting of 2 January 1832 it was agreed that the subject must be formally broached to the King, and the following day Grey journeyed down to Brighton. He asked William to create a small number of peers immediately, in order to indicate to the Lords what they could expect if they maintained their opposition. If this proved insufficient to force them into submission, a second batch could then be made.

The King responded in a memorandum of 5 January. He said that his doubts that an alternative administration could be formed in the event of his ministers' resignation, and his belief that the tranquillity of the country depended on a speedy settlement of the reform issue, meant that he did not altogether bar the possibility of creating peers to achieve such a settlement. To his consent, however, would be attached an irrevocable condition: the peerages should only be conferred on those who were already heirs to a title. In this way, the hereditary structure of the House of Lords would be preserved and its numbers

would not be permanently increased. Furthermore, he rejected Grey's project of creating a preliminary batch of peers as a demonstration to the Upper House. If creation were resorted to at all, a sufficient number of peers should be ennobled all at once rather than 'beating about the bush' with irresolute measures.

The King's ministers were delighted with this missive. Lord Holland said it showed there would be 'no more trouble' about creation. They were not, however, in a position to take immediate advantage of the King's implied consent. As yet they could not estimate how many new peers would ultimately be required to secure a majority in the Upper House. They therefore asked the King for a commitment that he would create as many peers as they required when they deemed it necessary. On 15 January 1832 the King agreed to this: in the last extremity he would create peers sufficient to satisfy 'the full exigency of the case'. He stressed, however, that his original condition that only heirs to existing titles should be elevated to

A cartoon by John Doyle alluding to the pressures surrounding the King during the Reform Bill crisis. In the background the courtiers are apprehensively watching Brougham who is closeted with the King after dinner at Windsor. He is seeking to persuade the King to agree to a creation of peers. William, however, is deaf to his appeals, peacefully slumbering through the audience.

the peerage in the event of a creation was still very much in force. William's commitment to his ministers was extensive but not unlimited.

Nevertheless, in the next few months William came to regret that he had gone so far. He had assumed, when giving his promise, that no more than about twenty-five peers would ultimately be required. This soon appeared to have been optimistic. Lord Wharncliffe warned that even those moderate peers who were at the moment inclined to compromise by supporting the new Reform Bill would be driven by a measure so drastic as a creation of peers into unremitting hostility to the Government. In these circumstances anything less than a very extensive addition to the peerage would prove inadequate. The thought appalled William: 'The step might ... have been resorted to, twenty-five or thirty peers added, and the Bill might still be lost', he lamented to Grey in February 1832. Grey did little to reconcile William to the prospect facing him. He constantly stressed that even if the Bill passed its second reading in the Lords, an addition to the peerage might still be necessary to prevent the insertion of catastrophic amendments in committee, and he positively wallowed in gloomy assurances that a creation would be repugnant to all men of good sense. Indeed, he even forwarded to William a copy of a letter which he had written to Lord Althorp, in which he referred to peer-making as 'a certain evil and ... very uncertain of success'. If even the arch-proponent of reform could speak of a creation in such unenthusiastic terms, it is hardly surprising that the arguments of its opponents were even more persuasive. The royal family were assiduous in arguing against the King exercising his prerogative on behalf of his ministers. 'All the royal family, bastards and all, have been incessantly *at* the King', Mr Greville noted in his diary, and the Queen in particular abandoned any semblance of discretion in her desire to dissuade the King from so disastrous a course. It was perhaps partly on account of her intrigues that, at some time in the spring of 1832, the belief that a Tory administration could act as a feasible alternative Government to the Whigs began to germinate in the mind of the King. By April 1832 Brougham believed that 'plotters' in the opposition had 'contrived to let the King know what they are prepared to do'. Lord Howe may have provided the channel of communication. Certainly in March he had written to Wellington, 'Pray my dear Duke, DEPEND UPON THE KING. Assure your party, if they will be *staunch*, he will be so.' If Wellington gave him an encouraging reply it may well have reached the King's ears. All these factors helped to contribute to the King's growing recalcitrance at the thought of creation. On 30 March 1832 he sent Grey an ominous letter in which, although referring to his promise to create a certain number of peers as 'sacred', he stated that he might not 'think fit to sanction' too many.

In these circumstances it was hardly likely that the King could be induced to enlarge on his original commitments to his ministers. Yet Lord Grey's assessment of the political situation constrained him to ask this of William. On 1 April 1832 Grey warned the King that it might be necessary to create between fifty and sixty peers to ensure that the Bill emerged from the Lords in recognizable form. But such a number could not be drawn exclusively from the ranks of those who were already heirs to a peerage. Several commoners were on the list of possible candidates that Grey submitted to William. He hoped that since the King had conceded the principle of creating peers he would not withdraw his support from his ministers over details such as this. He was to be disappointed. On 7 April the King indicated that he would never consent to the ennoblement of the commoners.

On 9 April the Lords began to debate the second reading of the Reform Bill. After an exhausting four-day sitting it was passed by a majority of nine. The King was delighted at the result, which he hoped had relieved him from the necessity of creating peers. Lord Albemarle said he became 'like a boy in spirits and delight' when he heard the news. But the victory was not conclusive. The opposition reunited in committee, and on 7 May a majority of the House voted to postpone discussion of the disfranchisement clause. The Government could not accept this. On 8 May Grey and Brougham sped down to Windsor to make a final desperate appeal to the King, begging him to create not less than fifty new peers, including some commoners. On the following morning the King gave them his refusal and accepted his ministers' resignations.

The King was aware that public opinion would not tolerate

the abandonment of reform, but he hoped that the Whigs could be replaced with an administration both prepared to introduce an 'extensive' measure of reform and capable of piloting it through the House of Lords. Initially he pressed Lord Brougham and the Duke of Richmond to stay in office and add their prestige to a new Government. Both refused. Peel also declined to head or even participate in an administration pledged to reform, for he indicated that if he did so he would lose all credibility as a man of principle. Surprisingly, the Duke of Wellington proved more flexible. For him, service to the crown was paramount. The King was in need of new servants; to refuse to assist him was unthinkable. The Duke told Alexander Baring that 'he should think himself unfit to crawl on earth, if he did not stand by the King, even at the expense of his own consistency', and added that he had resolved to carry the Reform Bill 'in all its great provisions'.

His difficulties in forming an administration would anyway have been manifold, but the task was further complicated by the wave of indignation that had surged through the public on the

A cartoon by John Doyle entitled 'Up and Down' or 'The Political See-Saw'. At the end of the 'days of May', Grey, with a little help from John Bull, is very much in the political ascendancy, while Wellington can do little but shout warnings to the King from his end of the see-saw. In the middle William struggles to maintain a balance.

resignation of the Whigs. At the end of his career Lord John Russell asserted that the so-called 'days of May' were the only moment of real peril to Britain that he could recall in his life. Mass meetings were held all over the country, and petitions signed by thousands poured in to Westminster. Trade ground to a halt, there was a run on gold and a threatened refusal to pay taxes. The fact that resistance was as yet confined to these passive measures seemed to many a sinister indication: 'All seemed reserved', Sir Robert Heron recorded, 'for a tremendous explosion.' Much of the public odium devolved upon the King, whose refusal to create peers was represented as an act of grossest perfidy. He drove up from Windsor on 12 May through a hissing crowd.

On 14 May an excitable House of Commons assembled. In a succession of bitter speeches the Whigs rose to indicate that, despite their contempt for what they regarded as the Tories' dishonourable manoeuvres, they would vote for reform regardless of who had introduced it. But the back-bench Tories could not be induced to render their leaders even this kind of support: Sir Robert Inglis and Davies Gilbert made stirring speeches denouncing the adoption of reform as entailing a shabby sacrifice of principle. When the House rose the leading Tories drove to Apsley House and told the Duke that a new administration was impossible. Baring said 'he would face a thousand devils rather than such a House of Commons'. On the morning of 15 May the Duke of Wellington offered his resignation to the King.

It seemed patently obvious that these developments had left the King no room to manoeuvre and that he must now take back Lord Grey on the latter's terms. It was therefore with an apparent total disregard of political realities that William wrote to Grey asking him to resume the premiership and to introduce a modified Reform Bill. Hardly surprisingly, Grey responded that this was impossible, and that he could only return to office on the explicit condition that an unspecified number of peers should be created should he deem it necessary. The King reacted indignantly. 'He is aware that gross misrepresentations of his conduct have gone abroad, that he is accused of having betrayed his ministers, and of having forfeited his pledge to them', he fumed bitterly, insisting that in fact his dealings with his

The interview between Lord Brougham, Lord Grey and the King, at which the latter was finally prevailed upon to consent to an unlimited creation of peers. Lord Brougham later described it as 'one of the most painful hours I have ever suffered in my life'. In his distress, the King kept his ministers standing while he himself remained seated.

ministers had been characterized by such scrupulous honesty that he saw no reason for them now to impose humiliating restrictions on his freedom of action. Patiently Grey agreed that he would defer specifying the conditions on which he resumed office until 18 May, in the hopes that by that date the Lords would have shown a more conciliatory disposition, and that the need for tampering with their membership would be obviated. To increase the chances of this solution, the King asked Taylor to write to Wellington asking him to declare that he had dropped his opposition to reform. Yet even while the King was seeking to moderate the attitude of the Lords, his eldest son was intriguing to stiffen them in their opposition. On 16 May he wrote to the Duke of Buckingham, 'The King repeated to me ... *that nothing should make him create peers. He is most stout.*' These communications may have encouraged the Lords to maintain their intransigence. At all events the tone in the Lords was so hostile on 17 May that the ministers agreed that the King must pledge himself to creating an unlimited number of peers if required. On 18 May Brougham and Grey had an audience with the King. Brougham later recalled, 'It was one of the most painful hours I ever suffered in my life because the King evidently suffered much, and yet behaved with greatest courtesy to us'. Uniquely, however, the King kept his ministers standing while he remained seated. When his ministers pressed him for a commitment on the peer question he replied with dignity, 'Well, now it must be so, and I consent'. To his annoyance Brougham asked him to commit his promise to paper. 'Do you doubt my word?' he muttered crossly, as he granted the request.

The peers were left in no doubt as to the consequences of continued opposition. Sir Herbert Taylor circulated a letter to the more prominent members of the opposition informing them exactly what they could expect. Abandoned by the King, they were forced to acknowledge defeat. Reluctantly, a majority agreed to absent themselves from reform divisions rather than risk a massive creation. The Bill was rushed through the committee in the Lords in only seven days, and on 4 June it passed its third reading by 106 votes to 22.

The King had been forced to concede to his ministers. He was not, however, prepared to endure a final indignity. When Grey

The Reform Bill receiving the royal assent by commission, as William himself refused to give it in person. This was perhaps fortunate, as when the King's representative gave the assent in the usual formula, 'le roi le veult', he received an anonymous note reading 'It would surely have been more appropriate if you had said "Le Canaille le veult"?'

suggested that he might regain some of his lost popularity by giving the royal assent to the Bill in person, the King returned an outright refusal. He fulminated that he 'had been misrepresented, calumniated and insulted' by the public in the past months. Was it expected that he should now 'cringe and bow' to those responsible? On 7 June the royal assent to the Bill was therefore given by commission, while William sulked at home. He should perhaps have comforted himself with the reflection that things could have been worse. However unwillingly, he had presided over a constitutional revolution. To have emerged suffering from little more than wounded pride was justifiable cause for self-congratulation.

165

7 King and Ministers

Never
when

THE KING'S INVOLVEMENT in domestic affairs did not preclude his monitoring of British foreign policy. On the contrary, he maintained an active and often intelligent interest in its conduct. The principles upon which he believed it should be formulated were straightforward. Fundamentally, his attitude was regulated by pure xenophobia. To Lord Melbourne he once wrote frankly, 'His Majesty is persuaded, as you are, that jealousy of the property and grandeur of this country is the dominant feeling of . . . every state on the continent.' Yet while the King entertained a robust distrust for the intentions of all foreigners, his suspicions of those of the French were particularly pronounced. He regarded the French King, Louis Philippe, as little more than a usurper, and for Talleyrand, the French Ambassador in London, he evinced an especial loathing. Occasionally the urgings of his ministers induced him to agree that British interests lay in co-operation with France, but nothing could shake his ingrained prejudice against the French character. 'His Majesty is not disposed to undervalue the importance of being upon good terms with France . . .' he assured Lord Grey in April 1832, 'but His Majesty does not trust France. He does not believe that she has abandoned her schemes of conquest and of extension of territory, or her designs of disturbing the tranquillity and the prosperity of other countries, by the propagation of revolutionary doctrines and principles.' It was indeed his association of France with radicalism that particularly sharpened his dislike, for in foreign affairs, as in domestic politics, William was an instinctive conservative. Princess Lieven summarized the factors that shaped his attitude as 'respect for royalty, hatred of new ideas'; certainly William had little sympathy for the constitutional and liberal movements on the Continent that were a feature of the 1830s. But despite his deference for such established monarchs as the sovereigns of Russia and Austria, he still viewed their activities on the diplomatic circuit with watchful suspicion, and was far from favouring a conjunction with the reactionary powers of Europe. He assured Lord Grey that even his mistrust of France could not induce him to 'support the arbitrary measures of a "Holy Alliance". He objects to that extreme almost as much as he does to the French system.'

For almost the whole of William's reign Lord Palmerston

preceding pages Contrary to William's hopes, the enthusiasm for reform did not die down with the passage of the Reform Bill. In this cartoon John Doyle depicts the Whigs driving the new reform coach at a reckless pace, while their passenger, the King, looks out anxiously.

A portrait of Viscount
Palmerston by Sir
Thomas Lawrence.
Throughout most of
William's reign
Palmerston was Foreign
Secretary, and the King's
strong views on the
conduct of foreign policy
did not always coincide
with those of his minister.

was Foreign Secretary. Palmerston did not necessarily view
world affairs in the same light as King William. To the King's
disgust, his suspicions of France were infinitely less exaggerated
than those of his master, and at times he displayed what William
regarded as a regrettable predilection for aiding constitutional
movements abroad. Fortunately the King respected Palmerston's abilities, and on occasion was forced to defer to his
superior intellect. Nevertheless, disagreement over questions of
foreign policy not infrequently served to inject an uncomfortable note of rancour into the King's relations with his ministers.

The first serious international problem which confronted the
King and his advisers was the question of Belgian independence,
a thorny issue which formed a constant background to the early
years of William's reign. In 1815 Belgium had been appor-

tioned to the Dutch, who governed the province with small regard for the fact that the Belgians' economic interests, religion and language differed from their own. The revolution in Paris had been swiftly followed by an uprising in Belgium, directed against her foreign masters. In November 1830 a conference of the European great powers was convened in London with the aim of settling the status of Belgium. Palmerston decided, and the King concurred, that since the union of Holland and Belgium had clearly failed, an independent Belgium must be established, free from the dominance of either their former masters, the Dutch, or their neighbours, the French. The conference accepted this and agreed that a King must be found for the Belgians. William's legitimist leanings led him to favour the candidacy of the Prince of Orange, son of the Dutch King. The Belgians, however, made it clear that such a choice would be quite unacceptable, and in February 1831 elected Louis Philippe's younger son as their King. In William's eyes this was a transparent manoeuvre by the French King to pave the way for the annexation of Belgium to France, and he fully endorsed Palmerston's insistence to the French that they must refuse the offer. When Palmerston suggested that Leopold of Saxe-Coburg, widower of Princess Charlotte, should be installed as King of the Belgians William was fleetingly concerned that the Dutch would suspect the British of wishing to establish a puppet King, dependent upon themselves. His suspicions of French intentions soon overrode these scruples, and with William's concurrence Leopold was offered the throne. The latter, however, refused to accept unless Luxemburg was freed from Dutch rule and awarded to Belgium. The Dutch King was so outraged by the conference's capitulation to this demand that he invaded Belgium in August 1831. To William's alarm, the French Army promptly went to the assistance of the Belgians and drove out all the invading forces, except for a small detachment which remained in the citadel of Antwerp. International pressure compelled the French to withdraw their troops also, but it was clear that a new solution to the Belgium question must be found to avoid further conflict. In October 1831 the London conference agreed on the twenty-four articles, a compromise arrangement that they hoped would satisfy both Belgium and Holland. To William's annoyance, the Dutch

Prince Leopold of Saxe-Coburg, afterwards King of the Belgians. He demanded that Belgium should be awarded Luxemburg before he agreed to accede to the Belgian throne.

170

King adamantly refused to accept the settlement. In the ensuing months, as Palmerston and the French sought to induce the King of Holland to yield, even William had to admit that the delay to a satisfactory conclusion to the negotiations was 'to be ascribed chiefly to the continued obstinacy and tergiversations of the King of the Netherlands'. Nevertheless, he shrank from the prospect of forcing the Dutch to submit by applying violent measures against them in conjunction with the French. 'His Majesty does not forget the hatred heaped upon Charles II and his ministry for assisting France against Holland', he wrote plaintively to Palmerston in the summer of 1832, and urged that only economic sanctions should be imposed on the Dutch. The Cabinet, however, decided that although the British should confine themselves to enforcing a naval blockade against Holland, French troops should march on the Dutch garrison at Antwerp. The King was gloomy about this plan, which he believed would be a prelude to the French occupation of the whole of Belgium, but having expressed his forebodings in six portentous sheets of memorandum he said he must bow to the unanimous wishes of the Cabinet. To his surprise, the Dutch at Antwerp surrendered after a month, and in May 1833, after nine months of economic blockade, the Dutch King agreed to abandon hostilities against the Belgians. The French forces withdrew, leaving Belgium truly independent. Even William was forced to admit grudgingly 'that the peace of Europe may have been mainly preserved by the concert of measures between England and France with respect to the Belgic question'.

Prince Metternich, the reactionary Austrian chancellor, painted by Sir Thomas Lawrence.

He was less inclined to relent upon Palmerston's policy towards the German states. In June 1832 the reactionary Austrian Chancellor, Metternich, had succeeded in forcing through the German Diet six resolutions intended to restrict further constitutional development in Germany, tightening censorship and preventing an enlargement of the franchise in the southern states. Palmerston disapproved of this repressive trend and was particularly displeased when William's representative as King of Hanover supported the resolutions in the Diet. Palmerston had no control over Hanoverian policy, but he knew that observers abroad believed that it was inspired by instructions from the British Foreign Office. William himself affirmed to Palmerston his approval of the six resolutions in

July, but the latter decided to give a public indication of his own position by asserting in the House of Commons that the welfare of constitutional states would always be a matter of concern to Englishmen. He followed this up by despatching, despite William's disapproval, a note to the President of the Diet attacking the six resolutions. The King was enraged. He enquired furiously of Palmerston whether he wished the press in other countries 'to become, as it is *here*, the governing power, bidding defiance to law and to every rule of society'? Palmerston was undaunted. The following year he asked William to instruct his Hanoverian ministers to decline an invitation to a conference of German states convened by Metternich. William refused, explaining that he did not wish to offend Austria, upon whom Hanover might depend for her future security. He added that, although he hoped that the conference would not result in the erosion of existing constitutional privileges in Germany, he had no wish to see them expanded. When the conference took place Palmerston could do nothing to prevent the Hanoverian delegates from firmly aligning themselves with Austrian policy.

Conflicting opinions about the situation in Portugal were to prove another cause of tension at home. The tyrannical and cruel Miguel had usurped the Portuguese throne from his niece, and her father, Pedro, was fighting to re-establish her rights. Palmerston shared the majority of the Whig party's abhorrence for the barbarities perpetuated by Miguel throughout his realm, but prudence forced him to declare an official policy of British neutrality to the conflict. This pleased William, who, according to Princess Lieven, held 'the little Queen's cause in detestation because it smacks of radicalism'. Nevertheless, Palmerston did the little that he could to help Pedro. When Pedro mounted an invasion of Portugal from the Azores, Palmerston ensured that the British fleet kept a benevolent eye on the proceedings. At first the invasion fared disastrously, but in July 1832 Pedro's forces succeeded in establishing a foothold in Oporto. The following year, after a brilliant victory at sea under Captain Napier, a British adventurer formerly in the Royal Navy, Pedro managed to capture Lisbon. William was enraged by Napier's interference in favour of young Donna Maria. During a royal visit to an exhibition at Somerset House, the President of

Charles Napier, the British adventurer whose victory at sea enabled the supporters of Donna Maria of Portugal to seize Lisbon. Napier was anathema to William, and the mere mention of his name once served to provoke a violent outburst from the King.

the Royal Academy had the ill luck to point out Napier's portrait and remark guilelessly, 'That is one of our naval heroes.' The King was transfixed with fury. 'Captain Napier may be damned sir, and you may be damned sir, and if the Queen was not here I would kick you downstairs sir!' he roared at the unfortunate official. Despite these strong feelings, the King was perforce obliged to acquiesce in the recognition of Donna Maria's Government, and his feelings towards her were anyway softened by the intelligence that Louis Philippe had snubbed the young Queen. When she visited England in 1833

Queen Maria II of Portugal and her husband, Ferdinand. William was not impressed by the young Queen when he met her, dismissing her as 'hideously ugly and rather stupid', but nevertheless he was prevailed upon to agree that the British should assist her cause.

the King agreed to entertain her at Windsor. The visit was not a great success from the personal angle – William later described Donna Maria as 'hideously ugly and rather stupid' – but Grey happily reported to Brougham that the King had 'conducted himself . . . with perfect discretion' throughout her stay. In January 1834 Pedro appealed to the British to intervene in Portugal in favour of his daughter's cause, and Grey actually managed to prevail upon the King to agree to a favourable response. On this occasion it was not the truculence of William but dissension within the Cabinet that prevented the sending of aid to Pedro, and the project was temporarily abandoned. But in April 1834 an alliance was signed between England, France, Spain and Portugal, pledging to restore peace in the Iberian peninsula. Later in the year Miguel surrendered to a British Admiral and retired to spend the rest of his life pensioned off in Rome. Despite this favourable conclusion to the Civil War, William insisted that he had countenanced intervention 'not indeed from any predilection for Don Pedro, or from any desire to encourage the introduction of a constitutional form of government . . .' but because the continued sovereignty of Miguel might have constituted a threat to British interests.

The Quadruple Alliance of April 1834 also involved England in the Civil War that was raging in Spain. There, another wicked uncle, Don Carlos, was seeking to wrest the throne from his young niece Isabella. Britain agreed to afford Isabella cautious assistance. Palmerston arranged that a force of British volunteers should be permitted to fight in Spain. Unfortunately, to command this British Legion he selected Colonel de Lacy Evans, the radical MP for Westminster, an individual of whom King William violently disapproved. This circumstance, combined with the fact that the policy of assisting Isabella had been forged in conjunction with France, contrived to ensure that his ministers found the King at his most refractory with regard to Spanish affairs. He proved extraordinarily obstinate about distributing honours to members of the British Legion, and when, in 1836, a fairly liberal constitution was forced upon the young Queen, he was hopeful that this absolved Britain of her treaty obligations. Even in 1837 Melbourne had considerable difficulty in persuading the King to renew the order-in-council which permitted the enlistment of British troops in Spain. In essence, the King could not believe the Spaniards merited such efforts on their behalf. In 1835 he grumbled that in his opinion all Spanish Governments were 'so incapable, so inefficient, so little consistent in principle, and almost invariably so ill-served' that he could see little point in becoming involved in their affairs. For William, even the most limited intervention in Spain represented a futile exercise in knight errantry.

William's and Palmerston's views largely coincided in their assessment of the threat posed by Russia's ambitions in eastern Europe. But this was the area of foreign affairs which William claimed afforded him the least satisfaction. The Turkish empire was in the process of disintegration and a former vassal of the Sultan's, Mehemet Ali, was exploiting the opportunity to carve out large chunks of it for himself. The Sultan appealed to Britain to aid him against Mehemet Ali's depredations, and both Palmerston and William were strongly in favour of a positive response to his request. The Cabinet were more cautious and blocked the proposal. The Sultan was obliged to turn for assistance to the Tsar, who was infinitely more forthcoming. In gratitude for Russia's help, the Sultan concluded the Treaty of Unkiar-Skelessi which guaranteed to Russia that the Dardanelles would be closed to all foreign warships in event of war. To William this was profoundly unsatisfactory. Although the tense situation in eastern Europe did not escalate into conflict during his reign, the King could detect that Russia's growing influence in that area constituted a real menace to British interests. In a memorandum of 1835 he growled that 'notwithstanding all her professions of moderation and disinterestedness with regard to the Porte, Russia . . . never will lose sight of her ambitious project in that quarter'. Like many of William's observations on foreign affairs, his analysis was in part inspired by simple chauvinism but at the same time it had a certain penetration.

The King's deeply ingrained mistrust of all foreigners meant that he acknowledged as a matter of course that Britain's stance towards foreign powers must be one of constant vigilance to prevent a devious encroachment upon her power. In domestic politics, however, he had hoped that a harmonious period of relaxation would follow the Reform Bill. These sanguine

above Colonel de Lacy Evans, the radical MP for Westminster whom Palmerston chose to lead the British legion fighting the Carlists in Spain. The King regarded de Lacy Evans as a dangerous firebrand, and this contributed to his hostility to the policy of assisting Queen Isabella.

below Queen Isabella II of Spain. Her Uncle Carlos claimed that she was debarred from the throne of Spain by virtue of Salic law and sought to gain it for himself.

expectations induced a notable improvement in his disposition in the summer of 1832. Lord Frederick Fitzclarence told Hobhouse in August, 'Matters were going on well at court. They had been very uncomfortable, but now were going on quiet and the King in good humour.' Unfortunately the situation was far from permanent. To the ministers it was transparently obvious that the passage of the Reform Bill entailed the necessity for a dissolution of Parliament and a fresh general election. The old Parliament had been returned under a system which had been declared obsolete; the electorate must be allowed to exercise their rights. William refused to admit the penetrating logic of this argument. He believed that all elections were periods 'of disorder, of general relaxation, and more or less of outrage'. To encourage this ferment wantonly would be inexcusable. His ministers complained that on this point the King was 'more obstinate and wrong-headed than they had ever found him'. Only the threat of a mass ministerial resignation compelled him to submit to their demand for dissolution, and he did so ungraciously. 'I yield, but, my Lords and gentlemen, remember it is against my opinion and wishes', he announced balefully. In the event the elections were not notable for any particularly violent excesses. The Whigs won an impressive 320 seats and the radicals failed to dominate the polls to the extent that pessimists such as William had predicted. Nonetheless, about 190 of them were returned to the new Parliament, and their presence, combined with that of 150 Tories, promised that the approaching session would be far from placid. Unfortunately Lord Grey seemed to have lost the will to endure a further trial in politics. After the Reform Bill his response to even fairly minor setbacks tended to be the offer of his resignation. When the Government lost a thinly attended division on the Malt Tax, or when the Cabinet refused to sanction intervention in Portugal, he showed himself disconcertingly ready to return to private life. Only the earnest entreaties of the King, who had come to respect and trust Grey, and the pleas of his colleagues kept him reluctantly in office. But with the question of Irish Church reform emerging to dominate and embitter British politics, it appeared increasingly doubtful that Grey would long tolerate the strain of leadership.

In Ireland the overwhelming majority of the inhabitants

were catholic, but the established Protestant Church neverthe-less flourished as an institution. It boasted a sumptuous structure of dioceses and benefices entirely disproportionate to the number of people it served. The catholic Irish peasant, barely able to support himself and his family, was obliged to contribute to the upkeep of an alien Church through the payment of tithes. Recent developments ensured that the iniquitous situation could no longer be ignored. Since the grant of catholic emancipation, an increasing number of catholic Irish members had been returned to Westminster, headed by the radical O'Connell. They forcefully demanded redress of their constituents' grievances. In 1831 protests against the payment of tithes had been so violent that they had had to be collected with the aid of troops and police, and since that time Ireland had remained in an abandoned and lawless condition. Clearly something had to be done, but the remedies proposed varied according to political outlook. Those on the left of the political spectrum, ranging from the demagogue O'Connell to the aristocratic Lord John Russell, proposed a complete overhaul of the Irish Church establishment, seeking to still protest by conciliation. To the more cautious this seemed a fearful solution, paving the way for further attacks on the Church and setting a dangerous precedent in undermining the rights of

A scene in Ireland: the visit of the tithe-proctor. Despite the fact that the majority of the Irish were Roman Catholics they were obliged to contribute financially to the upkeep of the Anglican Church through tithe payments. Efforts to collect the tithes, however, met with increased hostility from the impoverished peasants.

property. King William shared these fears, which were sharpened by a violent antipathy to O'Connell, whom he deemed a dangerous agitator. Grey himself was cautious about proceeding too fast in Ireland, and in 1833 brought the Cabinet to accept a compromise solution. Order would be restored in Ireland by force: a Coercion Bill would be passed permitting emergency measures to be adopted there. Simultaneously a Bill providing for a modest reform of the established Church should be introduced. Ten bishoprics were to be abolished, protestant clergy gradually withdrawn from exclusively catholic parishes and tithes commuted. To Lord Russell's annoyance, however, the clause in the Bill whereby the Church revenue thus saved should be devoted to lay purposes, such as education, was abandoned. Even so, the remaining provisions appeared to be meat too strong for the tender stomachs of the Lords. Throughout the spring of 1833 the Duke of Cumberland was busily, and apparently successfully, engaged in organizing resistance to the proposed measure among his fellow peers. The Government warned the King that should they not carry both the Coercion Bill and the Irish Church Bill they would resign. Although the King was hardly a partisan of Irish Church

above After 1831, resistance to the payment of tithes became both more organized and more violent, and troops and police who were called out to assist the tithe collectors could do little to contain events. The troubled conditions in the Irish countryside resulted in repressive legislation being enacted at Westminster.

overleaf The Reformed House of Commons in 1833. In January of that year a House of Commons elected under the reformed system assembled for the first time. This is one of the last pictures of the old Houses of Parliament, which were burnt to the ground in 1834.

181

'The Upsetting of the Reform Coach' – a cartoon by John Doyle. Stanley, Graham, Richmond and Ripon have all fallen off the coach after John Russell's declaration that the surplus revenues of the Irish Church should be appropriated for lay purposes. But coach has not halted, and its unwilling passenger, the King, calls from the window for help.

reform, he felt strongly that the stability of Lord Grey's Government must be his overwhelming priority. In June 1833 he therefore wrote to the Archbishop of Canterbury rebuking him for his opposition to the Government on a foreign policy question, in the hope that the reprimand would make him try to moderate his fellow prelates' unremitting hostility to Government measures. The ploy was ineffective: the Archbishop neglected to transmit the communication to his colleagues. To William's acute distress, the Lords' threatened intransigence resulted in the resurrection of a dreaded spectre: Brougham blithely suggested that a more pliant House of Lords should be secured through a limited creation of peers. The King complained incredulously that the Chancellor seemed to have forgotten the difficulties that had attended the last occasion when peer-making was in the offing. He admitted, however, that it was the Lords' irresponsibility that had provoked the crisis, and despairingly promised to renew his canvass of the episcopal bench with an appeal to the Archbishop of York. Fortunately a crisis was averted by the belated restoration of the Duke of Wellington's senses. He sternly informed his colleagues in the Lords that the Irish Church Bill must be permitted to reach the statute book for the sake of the Church itself, and their opposition crumbled.

But the question had not been despatched for long. In May 1834 Lord John Russell revived it by stating bluntly in debate that he believed that the surplus revenues of the Irish Church should be appropriated for lay purposes. This was too much for the more conservative members of the Government. Stanley, the former secretary for Ireland, scribbled ruefully to his colleague Graham, 'Johnny Russell has upset the coach'; later in the month Stanley, Graham, Ripon and Richmond baled out of the rattling conveyance altogether with the tender of their resignations. Grey was only prevented from following their example by the stern remonstrances of Brougham. The King too was gravely perturbed at the thought of a further onslaught on the Irish Church. He consented to the establishment of a commission of enquiry into its condition with the deepest of misgivings. His true feelings were discernible in his reply to a petition from the clergy deploring ecclesiastical innovations. 'The King, in answer, warmly expressed his attachment to the Church in which he had been educated', the Tory Duke of Buckingham recorded smugly. When the four outgoing ministers came to take their leave of the King he informed them that they had taken the correct course, and mourned that it was the four members of the Cabinet that he liked the best who were departing. At court it was noted that of late the King had become particularly irritable.

He was not the only one to feel the strain. Lord Grey wrote gloomily to Brougham, 'I feel more and more doubtful as to the possibility of our going on', and in July the renewal of the Irish Coercion Bill provided the occasion for his departure. O'Connell understood himself to have received a private undertaking from the Irish Secretary, Littleton, that the more offensive clauses of the Coercion Bill would be dropped upon its renewal. Lord Grey, however, had prevailed upon the Cabinet to agree that it must be re-enacted almost in its entirety. When, therefore, Grey re-introduced in the House of Lords a measure virtually identical to the last, O'Connell complained that he had been subjected to a breach of faith. In the wake of the ensuing recriminations and bitterness Lord Althorp resigned. Wearily, Grey did likewise.

The ministry, already weakened by the slow draining of moderate blood, had now been decapitated. It must either be remodelled or replaced altogether. Although still alarmed at the turbulent storms to be weathered if the Whigs remained at the political helm, the King conceded that he could not impose a Tory ministry on a largely unreceptive House of Commons. Lord Grey's recommendation of the urbane and moderate Lord Melbourne as his successor helped to reconcile the King to this unpalatable fact. Nevertheless, he was hopeful that the strong progressive medicine of the Whigs could be diluted with a dash of Tory caution. He requested Melbourne to approach both Peel and Wellington with proposals to form a coalition ministry. Melbourne was convinced that the differences between the parties were too great to be submerged in amicable co-operation, but he obediently complied with the King's request. As predicted, the replies returned by the Tory leaders were unconditional refusals. The King apparently took this setback with philosophical resignation: he told Lord Brougham that even if the negotiations foundered 'he will not regret having made the trial'. But the King's fears at the thought of excessive reform at the hands of the Whigs had not subsided. He forlornly asked Melbourne to guarantee that he would resist further encroachments upon the Church and State. Melbourne's courteous but reserved response fell far short of William's hopes in this respect.

The conduct of the Whigs over the next few months did little to reassure the King. In order to woo Lord Althorp back to office, the Government meekly lopped off the more controversial sections of the Coercion Act, in William's opinion a lamentable capitulation to radical pressure. Indeed, to the King's fearful eyes, the entire direction of the ministry seemed more inclined to the left than that of its predecessor. In the Commons the radicals generally supported the ministers, who now seemed to frame their policies with less regard to the sensibilities of the House of Lords. Yet ministerial prestige was undermined by their lack of any speaker of stature to parry the

186

thrusts of Stanley and Peel in debate. The principal business of the Government in the Commons devolved upon the conscientious but plodding Lord Althorp, 'the tortoise upon whom the world reposed'. The King's faith in his ministers was further undermined by the fact that Lord Brougham had succumbed to a bizarre attack of egoistic folly. His entire demeanour had recently been characterized by an overweening arrogance to both King and colleagues. 'He seemed to forget that the King was still his master', John Cam Hobhouse noted reprovingly. Then in August 1834 the Chancellor pranced off to Scotland and embarked on a flamboyant personal progress, marked by a series of impassioned and injudicious speeches. Invigorated by his reception and by whisky toddy, he penned the disapproving King a series of colourful letters detailing his triumph. Other, less indulgent, sources informed the King of the Chancellor's more unfortunate eccentricities. William learnt to his amazement that in the course of Brougham's peregrinations the Great Seal was on one occasion used as a prop in a parlour game. By the autumn the King's dislike of Brougham was common knowledge; *The Times* even informed its readers that 'the King makes no scruple of speaking of him as an itinerant mountebank, who has dragged the Great Seal of England through the kennel, and degraded, by his unnumbered antics and meannesses, the highest offices of the law and state in England'. To William it seemed that he was saddled with an immoderate ministry which commanded scant respect in the country, and which had been further discredited by the conduct of a demented Chancellor. His growing impatience at the predicament was to lead him into a serious error of judgement.

The Lord Chancellor, Lord Brougham. During the summer of 1834 his behaviour became increasingly eccentric. He infuriated the King by embarking on a pilgrimage of self-glorification through Scotland. William's displeasure at this contributed to his dissatisfaction with Lord Melbourne's Government.

In November 1834 Lord Althorp's father, Lord Spencer, died. His death entailed Althorp's transfer from the House of Commons to the House of Lords, and he had indicated that once installed in that 'hospital for incurables' he would cease to take an active part in government. Both Lord Grey and Lord Melbourne had implied that the Government depended for its survival upon Lord Althorp's diligent shepherding of the majority in the House of Commons. When, therefore, Lord Melbourne wrote to inform the King that he wished to see him at Brighton to discuss the implications of Spencer's death, William eagerly persuaded himself that the Premier had come to offer the collective resignation of his ministers. His interview with Melbourne on 13 November therefore came as something of a disappointment. Melbourne came not to resign but to propose that Lord John Russell should succeed Althorp as Leader of the House of Commons. To the King, Russell was anathema, branded a dangerous radical by his championship of Irish Church reform. Brusquely he observed that Russell would 'make a wretched figure' as Leader of the House. The King's refusal to consider any of Melbourne's other candidates for the post forced the Prime Minister to persist in requesting Russell's nomination. The King now came to the crux of the matter: he pointed out that Russell was pledged to a further reform of the Irish ecclesiastical establishment, and that the introduction of such a measure could not fail to precipitate a distressing clash between the King and his ministers. He feared, furthermore, that it would provoke further resignations within the administration, and that any vacancies thus incurred would be filled by radicals and undesirables. The King added darkly that 'the injudicious and extravagant conduct of Lord Brougham' had disturbed his confidence in the ministry. The shaken Melbourne appealed to the King to consider the future of his ministry overnight, but, although William agreed to avoid appearing arbitrary or unobliging, in reality he had already decided that the circumstances warranted the dismissal of his ministers. At dinner that night Lady Brownlow noted that the King was 'in great spirits and laughed heartily at Lord Adolphus' jokes'. The following day he informed Melbourne that he believed it would not be acting 'fairly or honourably' to ask him to continue in office under such inauspicious conditions. This consideration was indeed central to William's decision. A more subtle man might have bided his time in the hope that the Government would disintegrate of its own accord under the strains of its Irish policy. But to a man of the King's formidable integrity it seemed pointless and discreditable to extend his confidence hypocritically to his ministers, in the hope that their measures would soon land them in trouble. It was better to dismiss them amicably at once, before the atmosphere had been embittered by clashes on matters of specific policy.

Melbourne himself took the news of his dismissal very equably. As he was going back to town, he gallantly agreed that it might save time and trouble were he to convey the King's summons to the Duke of Wellington. In a letter to Grey he charitably commented, 'I am not surprised at the King's decision, nor do I know that I can entirely condemn it.' Yet this gentlemanly insouciance was by no means a universal reaction. In general the Whigs' response was one of outrage. Disappointed ambition led Brougham in particular to behave with ostentatious bad taste, sending the Great Seal back to the King wrapped up in a bag 'exactly as a fishmonger might have sent a salmon for the King's dinner'. Nor was censure confined to such indirect, if expressive, demonstrations: even before Melbourne had communicated the news to the majority of his colleagues, a scathing account of the ministers' summary dismissal appeared in *The Times* of 15 November, ending with the entirely unfounded comment, 'the Queen has done it all'. Edward Ellice, the Government Whip, was probably responsible for the disclosures and the unjust conclusion, but to the King it seemed a final confirmation of the Whigs' unreliability. On that morning he was in fact already in conference with the Duke of Wellington when Taylor brought in the paper and pointed out the offending paragraph. 'There Duke! You see how I am insulted and betrayed!' the King declaimed explosively. 'Will Your Grace compel me to take back people who have treated me in this way?' Wellington, although feeling that the King had acted prematurely, loyally promised his assistance. But he insisted that Sir Robert Peel must head any new administration, ruefully aware that a Prime Minister from the House of Lords could have little influence on an unruly House of Commons. Peel, however, was on holiday abroad, and the King pleaded that the Duke would at least take up the reins of government while Peel was summoned home. For a bizarre interlude, therefore, one man alone constituted virtually the entire Government of England. The Duke of Wellington encompassed the offices of First Lord of the Treasury, Home Secretary, Foreign Secretary and Secretary for War. The Whigs waxed indignant at Wellington's nominal monopoly of executive power – Lord Grey angrily dubbing the Duke 'His Highness the Dictator' – but with the return of Peel on 9 December the Duke thankfully surrendered his seals and entrusted to the younger man the arduous task of forming an administration.

overleaf, left Lord John Russell by Grant. The King intensely disliked Russell whom he deemed a dangerous radical, and to whom he always balefully referred as 'that young man'. Melbourne's suggestion that Russell should replace Lord Althorp as Leader of the House of Commons was one of the reasons why William decided to dismiss his Whig Government.

overleaf, right Lord Melbourne, Lord Grey's successor as William's Prime Minister. All his reserves of charm were called upon to handle his excitable master.

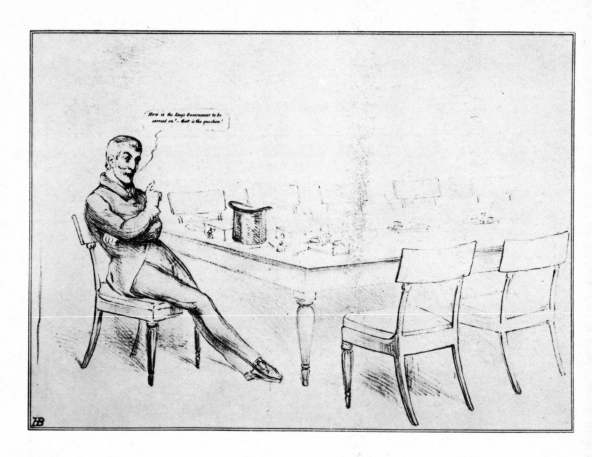

above In November 1834 the Duke of Wellington agreed to assume all the major cabinet offices until Peel returned from Rome to lead the Government. In this cartoon John Doyle depicts the Duke in debate with himself at the Cabinet table.

opposite Sir Robert Peel sought to appeal to voters by promising to espouse constructive reform where necessary. Nevertheless, the Tories could not survive combined onslaughts by Whigs and radicals in the House of Commons.

To Peel it seemed likely that the King had gravely miscalculated. Nevertheless he felt obliged to stand by the consequences of his sovereign's actions. He hoped to strengthen his position by including in his Government those moderates who had deserted the Whigs earlier in the year. His overtures to Stanley and Graham were, however, politely rejected, and Peel was left forlornly assembling an administration of committed Tories which he knew had little chance of survival in a House of Commons dominated by Whigs and radicals.

In an attempt to secure a more amenable House of Commons, Peel dissolved Parliament and appealed to the country. During the campaign he revealed a new positive aspect to the face of Toryism: in an address to his Tamworth constituents he emphasized that his party were prepared to embrace constructive reform where necessary. The results of the election were reasonably encouraging. The Tories gained at the expense of the Whigs, and, although the radicals held their ground, the

Tories emerged as the largest single party in the new House. But they could not command a majority against a united opposition, and this was what they had to face. In February 1835 the Whigs secured an informal agreement from the radicals that they would combine with them against the Government. This formidable partnership first showed its teeth when the opposition rejected the Tories' choice of speaker, traditionally an appointment devoid of controversy. In March parliamentary outcry against the selection of the reactionary Lord Londonderry as Ambassador to Russia forced him to relinquish his post. Mr Greville, unaccustomed to the concept of automatic opposition from those out of office, was shocked by such violence. In his diary he noted primly, 'It is the first time (as far as I know) that any great party ever proceeded upon . . . such a principle . . . namely to destroy the King's ministry without any reference to the measures that ministry may propose'. Predictably the reaction of the King was less measured. He had hoped that his own emphatic support, combined with the Tories' avowed determination not to obstruct reform blindly, would gradually persuade moderates in the Commons to abstain from factious opposition. As it became increasingly apparent that the hope had been illusory, William had to contemplate the humiliating possibility of an imminent Whig return to power. Should such an eventuality occur, he made it plain that he would submit to it as a matter of duty, but that his support would not extend beyond the most nominal of formalities. 'It is impossible that he can give his confidence to men so introduced into his councils,' he insisted to Peel, '. . . His Majesty might be obliged to *tolerate* them but he could not meet them cordially, nor communicate with them as friends. They may become his ministers, but never his *confidential* servants. He would receive all their advice with jealousy and suspicion . . .'

The Whigs, however, seemed to care little for the King's sensibilities. Lord John Russell had decided that the King must be humbled on the very ground that had formed the specific basis for his dismissal of the Whig ministry – the disestablishment of the Irish Church. Russell managed to carry successive resolutions against the Tories, establishing that the surplus revenues of the Irish Church should be applied for lay purposes and that any future Government Bill relating to Irish tithes must necessarily incorporate this principle. Peel could not endure such humiliations indefinitely. By late March only the exhortations of the Duke of Wellington kept him in office. The strain of sustaining repeated defeats at last became insupportable, and on 8 April he resigned. Desperately, the King appealed to Grey to return to office to relieve him of the necessity of crawling back to the ministers he had so jauntily dismissed. Firmly Grey indicated that there was no alternative but recourse to Melbourne.

For the King it was a bitter pill. He had exerted no more than his constitutional rights in seeking to rid himself of Whig governance and Whig reform. But he had grossly overplayed his hand. Royal ability to manipulate the House of Commons had been dwindling for nearly half a century. To expect that the crown could exert a persuasive influence there, even after the Reform Bill had struck at its remaining sinews of patronage, was illusory indeed. Yet it was hardly likely that the knowledge that he had been made ridiculous would make the King any more disposed to co-operate with the ministers who had been foisted upon him. William might be firmly in the Whig cage, but it seemed all too probable that he would seek to incommode his jailers by ferociously rattling at the bars.

8
The Final Phase

FROM THE START, Lord Melbourne made it plain that he was not prepared to tolerate much nonsense on the part of William, requiring certain undertakings from the King before he consented to resume his responsibilities. Melbourne established that in future all officers of the royal household would be required to give unequivocal support to the Government in Parliament. Furthermore, he firmly contradicted the King's assertion that he should have the right to prevent office being awarded to individuals of whom he particularly disapproved. Yet, while not prepared to concede the principle, Melbourne showed himself disposed to accommodate the King on detail, provided it could be done without compromising the integrity of his Government. He himself had no wish to include radicals and extremists in his administration, and when he learnt through Lord Grey that the King abhorred the promotion of only three individuals – O'Connell, Sheil and Hume – he was able to give the King an informal assurance that they would not be imposed on him. William was not even subjected to renewed dealings with Brougham, an ordeal to which he probably would have submitted as a disagreeable necessity had not Melbourne already resolved that Brougham was too intolerable a colleague to merit office.

One problem, however, remained. The King still refused to commit himself to sanctioning a further reform of the Irish Church. Melbourne remorselessly insisted that he must have an undertaking to this effect, pointing out that his party was effactually pledged to such a measure. Still the King wriggled on the hook. He protested that by consenting to the despoilation of the Irish Church he might violate his coronation oath, and proposed to refer the matter to a panel of fifteen judges for their consideration. Melbourne crisply retorted that such a course would be 'highly inexpedient', observing sharply that the question was one 'not of law but of conscience, and upon which the opinion of judges is worth no more than that of other men'. Reluctantly, however, he agreed that the King might approach the Tory Chancellor, Lord Lyndhurst, for a judgement on the subject. Lyndhurst resolutely avoided becoming embroiled in so contentious an issue. 'The Lord Chancellor positively declines giving any opinion *whatsoever* to the King', William wrathfully informed Melbourne. In the face of this final setback

preceding pages William IV towards the end of his life, in a drawing by Richard Easton.

198

the King's resistance collapsed. As it turned out, his struggle had been unnecessary. Later in the year the Whigs introduced an Irish Tithe Bill with a clause providing for the appropriation of surplus Church revenue for lay purposes. The Lords amended it so drastically that the ministers decided to drop the entire Bill. The following year the process was repeated, and in 1837 the Lords suffered a similar Bill to pass only on condition that the appropriation clause was forfeited. In consequence, the Irish Tithe Bill, so dreaded by the King, emerged from the Lords in a disarmingly innocuous condition.

Yet William could not foresee these happy developments. In April 1835 he only knew that a ministry of whose projected

Although William had been obliged to accept the Whigs' return to power, they had been weakened by Tory successes in the General Election. Much to the displeasure of the King, they had therefore to rely on the votes of the Irish radicals, headed by Daniel O'Connell. Here the Whigs Ebrington and Duncannon are seen entertaining O'Connell at Brooks's Club.

policies he violently disapproved had been thrust upon him. The Duchess of Gloucester, the King's sister and confidant, reported that William was in 'the most pitiable state of distress, constantly in tears and saying that "he felt his crown tottering on his head"'. In June the King was still maintaining a wall of sullen resentment against the Whigs. When Adolphus Fitzclarence enquired of his father whether he would be entertaining on the usual scale during Ascot week, the King replied irritably, 'You know I cannot give a dinner; I cannot give any dinners without inviting the ministers, and I would rather see the devil than any one of them in my house'. If the King had reluctantly accepted that he could not rid himself of his ministers, he was at least determined that they should derive no pleasure from their position.

That the situation in the next two years did not become completely intolerable for both King and ministers owed much to the fact that Melbourne displayed a dexterous mixture of tact and firmness when handling his sovereign. John Cam Hobhouse was to speak admiringly of 'the good sense and good manners of our chief, who knew how to deal with his master', while Melbourne himself later asserted that the King had liked him 'as much as anybody could under the circumstances'. This was not due solely to the exercise of Melbourne's famous charm: William appreciated that Melbourne was the most tepid of reformers, and accepted that if he had to have a Whig Government it was in his interests that Melbourne headed it. The King even honoured Melbourne with the tribute that he believed him 'to be a *conservative* in the truest sense of the word, and to as great a degree as is His Majesty himself'. But while the King did not fear Melbourne's own intentions he did doubt his Prime Minister's ability to impose his moderate opinions on his colleagues. As for Melbourne himself, he was later to give Sir Herbert Taylor much credit for the maintenance of the uneasy equilibrium between King and ministers. 'The King used to go and talk to Taylor, and Taylor softened matters', Melbourne was later to reminisce to Queen Victoria. With characteristic generosity, the Prime Minister was also to commend William's own moderation under difficult circumstances. 'He once or twice did things which embarrassed us a good deal,' Melbourne admitted to Victoria, 'but on the whole he was very fair.'

200

This was perhaps excessively charitable. Since he had no alternative to a Whig ministry, the King should ideally have made a consistent effort to master his feelings of antipathy to the Government. Instead he showed himself on occasion both churlish and obstructive. As his control over policy had virtually lapsed, his interventions were almost invariably futile, but that did not make them any the less harassing for his ministers. At times, indeed, the King nearly goaded them beyond endurance, only narrowly avoiding provoking them into resignation, which would have resulted in a serious constitutional crisis. In June 1835, for example, William reacted to Palmerston's failure to consult him about appointing Durham Ambassador to Russia with such intemperate abuse of his Foreign Secretary that Melbourne commented ominously, 'I know not how I can acquiesce under it'. The Prime Minister managed to placate the King, but the following month another disagreeable incident arose. William shared the fears of conservatives throughout the ages of an invasion by Russia. He informed John Russell that 'Russia had 100,000 men ready for embarkation in the Baltic; he did not know how his Lordship felt but he owned they made him shake in his shoes'. In these circumstances he would regard any proposal to reduce the militia as parsimonious lunacy. Unfortunately, this was exactly what his ministers had in mind. In September the question was broached in Council, prompting the King to burst out, 'My Lords, I am an old man – older than any of your Lordships – I therefore know more than any of you', and he followed this confident assertion with a lengthy harangue, warning that in the next session of Parliament he would reverse any steps taken to reduce the militia, 'whoever may be, or whoever are, ministers'. Wisely the ministers declined to take issue with this disquisition, Melbourne confining himself to looking 'very black and very haughty'.

Further disagreements revolved around the governance of Canada. The ministers were considering liberalizing the administration of the dependency, but to William this seemed the most reprehensible folly. When Sir Charles Grey, one of the commissioners selected to inquire into the affairs of Canada, was sworn in at the Palace the King suddenly launched into an agitated effusion, reminding him that Canada was 'not an original possession of the Crown, but that it was obtained *by the sword*'. Sir Charles should therefore 'take care to assert those undoubted prerogatives which the Crown there possesses and . . . of which persons who ought to have known better have dared even in my presence to deny the existence'. This last oblique reference turned out to have been a swipe at the Minister for the Colonies, Lord Glenelg, for whom the King had entertained a potent hatred since 1830 when he had blocked a financial grant to the Queen. The Cabinet decided that such an outburst could not be tolerated, Melbourne describing it as 'a mass of muddle and impropriety such as never, probably, was equalled before', and they drew up a remonstrance to be laid before the King. William received it in an apparently penitent frame of mind: Melbourne reported proudly that the King had 'admitted the full force of my observations, and felt that he had said more than he ought to have said'. It was, apparently, an ephemeral triumph. Only a few days later the King burst out to Lord Gosford, Governor-designate of Canada, 'mind what you are about in Canada . . . mind me, my Lord, the Cabinet is not my Cabinet; they had better take care or by God, I will have them impeached'. The Cabinet elected to ignore this announcement. At heart William himself knew that such ebullitions were to be deprecated. After he had yet again been rude to Glenelg during a consultation in the closet, the King enquired nervously of Melbourne if Lord Glenelg had found him uncivil. When the Premier coldly indicated that he had indeed, William made an especial effort to be good humoured with Glenelg at his next interview. His outbursts were not the product of a preconceived plan to force his ministers into resignation, but rather the spontaneous products of prolonged frustration. They were, however, only marginally less unfortunate for that.

Municipal reform provided another focus for hostility between William and his Government. The corporations which presided over the administration of Britain's towns were notoriously corrupt and incompetent oligarchies. Since 1833 a commission had been investigating them, and on the basis of its report the Whigs formulated a sweeping measure of reform, designed to make away with 200 old councils and replace them with 179 municipal boroughs controlled by elective corporations. Predictably, William was alarmed by such comprehensive proposals, objecting particularly to the abolition of established councils and to the lowness of the proposed municipal franchise. Melbourne assured the King that this was a reform that even he felt was particularly necessary, and William temporarily subsided, but when the Bill sailed through the Commons he grumbled that the House had paid scant attention to the 'judicious and necessary' amendments proposed by the opposition. The Bill was then submitted to the Upper House, where the Lords, no doubt heartened by reports of William's antagonism to the measure, gleefully proceeded to dismember the Bill. It returned to the Commons virtually unrecognizable, and once again the distressing prospect loomed of a clash between the two Houses. Collision was averted when men of good sense combined in the Commons to restore the Bill to acceptable form, Peel speaking forcefully in favour of the measure, and John Russell showing an unwonted disposition to compromise by agreeing to incorporate some of the Lords' less obnoxious amendments into the Bill. In this form the Lords were induced to pass the Bill. Despite his original objections to the measure, William could not but feel relief that a crisis had been deflected, and he even brought himself to send a letter to the hated Russell congratulating him on his moderation.

By the late autumn of 1835 William was becoming accustomed, if not reconciled, to the renewed tutelage of the Whigs, even inviting them to dine with him in November. This did not prevent him from indulging in spasmodic skirmishes with his ministers throughout 1836. He maintained a stubborn opposition to administrative evolution in Canada and was cantankerous over policy to Spain. The ministers were still sensitive about such outbursts. When William succumbed in August to the temptation of launching an attack at the head of 'the vacillating and procrastinating Lord Glenelg' for neglecting to award an honour to Lord Aylmer, Melbourne commented gloomily that the King seemed prepared to drive him to resign. 'Much allowance ought to be made for his infirmities of all kinds, but it will not do to bear too much', he concluded darkly. Nevertheless, in the interludes between these bouts of hostility the King showed himself at times almost cordial to his ministers. In May 1836 a correspondent informed Durham, 'His Majesty is very gracious to all the ministers, and, I understand, is quite content with them'. When Melbourne was accused of adultery with Mrs Norton the King refused to hear of his resignation, warmly congratulating him on his subsequent acquittal in the divorce proceedings. In November the ministers again received a heartening invitation to dine with the King 'and drink two bottles of wine a man'.

The King's more mellow frame of mind was in part due to the fact that he lacked the vitality to pursue a sustained vendetta against his ministers. In May 1836 an observer reported that the King was 'somewhat shrunk both in mind and body . . . After his dinner naps he wakes shaking and he is not so strong on his legs . . . The medical men about him consider the decay of age is fast coming upon him'. Although his declining health contributed to the King's irritability, it ensured that his outbursts were of comparatively short duration. It also ensured that his temper was quite indiscriminately directed against those who annoyed him. When Leopold of the Belgians dined at Windsor William was outraged to hear him decline the wine in preference for water. 'God damn it!' he bellowed down the table, 'Why don't you drink wine? I never allow anybody to drink water at my table.' The Whigs could draw perverse comfort from the fact that they were not the only victims of His Majesty's irascibility.

The lasting contentment afforded by his marriage helped to compensate the King for his infirmities. William had once said to Princess Lieven, 'I could never explain to you, Madam, the innumerable ways in which the Queen is of use to me', and his dependence on his wife had only increased with the years. Admittedly, when Adelaide had arranged to visit Meiningen in 1834, William had seemed quite excited at her imminent departure. He had roguishly enquired of a distinguished old Admiral 'whether he was as great a rascal as ever?' intimating gleefully that he was anticipating a return to the follies of his youth. Once the Queen had gone, however, his spirits had sunk. On her return Adelaide had found him ill, depressed and exhausted, and more devoted to her than ever. The company of his daughters also served to comfort the King in his old age. The eldest, Lady de l'Isle, was particularly attentive, tending him at Brighton in the winter of 1836 and driving with him every afternoon.

Queen Adelaide in later life. As the King grew older he became more devoted to his wife than ever.

His sons were not to give him the same succour. Despite the fact that William had annoyed the House of Commons by making his eldest son the Constable of the Round Tower and a Privy Councillor, Lord Munster continued to think himself ill-used. He gave the King great pain by his repeated and bitter complaints about his supposedly impoverished condition. The King was always seeking to mollify Munster but to no avail. When William offered to pose for a portrait for him his son only venomously retorted that this would be a pointless exercise as he would soon be obliged to pawn the painting. He responded to his father's inability to provide him with any further financial endowment by refusing to visit him at all.

Frederick Fitzclarence was a similar malcontent. He too complained that his father's financial arrangements had discriminated against him, expecting a larger share of William's wealth than his younger brothers and all his sisters. In February 1837 he rehearsed his grievances in a letter of such violence that Taylor declined to pass it on to the King, preferring instead to administer a stern reproof himself. 'Surely some credit and gratitude also are due to the King', Sir Herbert cogently urged, 'for having contrived, in little more than six years . . . to give to his children . . . nearly £30,000 each, besides their annual allowances.' Sadly, credit and gratitude seemed qualities almost entirely foreign to the Fitzclarence brothers. Augustus upset his father by peremptorily rejecting as inadequate the offer of a Prebendary at Worcester which had been painstakingly secured for him, and he refused to conduct his sister's marriage service because the ceremony was to be performed in one of his father's houses. He then complained that not enough had been done to further his career. Only Adolphus Fitzclarence honoured William with anything remotely approaching filial affection, a meagre reward indeed for one who had been such a conspicuously devoted father.

One other aspect of family affairs contrived to vex the King's declining years. William and Adelaide had once enjoyed a fairly warm relationship with their widowed sister-in-law, the Duchess of Kent. Adelaide, indeed, had proved a source of great comfort to the Duchess at the time of her bereavement. On William's accession to the throne, however, the Duchess, no doubt out of jealousy, chose to terminate their intimacy. Her bearing to William and Adelaide was henceforth unreasonably imperious. When Adelaide visited her at Kensington Palace she either kept the Queen waiting or refused to see her at all. Egged on by her scheming comptroller, Sir John Conroy, she made it clear that she believed that her position as mother to the future Queen entitled her to the most exaggerated deference. Frequently, indeed, she chose to act as if she were already Regent. The unfortunate Princess Victoria was the instrument she used to flaunt her disregard for the King and Queen.

William and Adelaide were dotingly fond of children, and were touchingly desirous to have frequent access to their niece. The Duchess, however, elected to prevent them meeting on a

The Duchess of Kent by Beechy. In the face of repeated provocation from his sister-in-law, William finally lost his patience and insulted her publicly at his birthday banquet.

regular basis. With insulting prudery she kept her and her daughter's visits to Windsor to a minimum, on the grounds that contact with the illegitimate Fitzclarences might somehow corrupt Victoria's purity. The Duchess sought to prevent her daughter from attending the royal drawing-rooms, and succeeded in keeping her away from the coronation by manufacturing a quarrel about precedence. By such contrivances she managed to deprive the King of the perfectly legitimate pleasure of friendship with his niece.

In 1832 the conflict between Kensington and Windsor entered a new phase as the Duchess embarked with her daughter on a stately progress through England. At a time when William's own standing in the country was at a low ebb because of the Reform Bill crisis, she drew offensive attention to the popularity of his niece. The Duchess even capitalized on the fact that, unlike most of the royal family, she was reputed to be in favour of reform by graciously accepting loyal addresses thanking her for her support of the 'free people' of England. Hardly surprisingly, William was infuriated by such exhibitions. Nevertheless, he was unable to prevent the Duchess from undertaking similar jaunts during the next two years. Even in 1835, when Victoria herself suggested that they should desist from the annual tour to avoid annoying the King, the Duchess and Conroy insisted that it must proceed.

Other grievances had meanwhile arisen. When the King told the Duchess that the royal yacht was at her disposal, she did not bother to acknowledge the offer, although she subsequently took full advantage of it. On her visits to the Isle of Wight she insisted that she was greeted with an imposing salvo of gun salutes, to which her position scarcely gave her entitlement. She refused to drop this ostentatious practice voluntarily, so that the King was obliged to prevent her from being saluted again by altering the regulations governing such matters. When two young Princes from Wurtemberg came to visit their cousin Victoria, William politely invited them to Windsor. The Duchess refused on the grounds that the Princes were otherwise engaged on the day appointed. The King subsequently learnt from the newspapers that on that afternoon the Princes had paid a visit to London Zoo.

By now the King detested his sister-in-law. Patience had never been his strongest suit, and at times the Duchess was made to pay for her insolence. At Victoria's confirmation in 1835 the King announced that her mother's entourage was too large, and commanded Sir John Conroy to leave the chapel. He also sought to thwart any plans the Duchess might nurse of selecting a husband for Victoria from among her Coburg relatives, determined that instead Victoria should marry Prince Alexander of Orange. When the Duchess invited Prince Albert of Saxe-Coburg to England in 1836 William even formally enquired of the Lord Chancellor whether he could prevent the Prince from landing. Melbourne indicated that such a course would be unwise, and William submitted to his judgement. In August 1836, however, he had ample revenge.

The Duchess had caused the King more than usual offence by declining to attend the Queen's birthday party, although she signified that she would grace that of the King a few days later. Before her visit William's temper was further frayed by the discovery that the Duchess had annexed a suite of seventeen rooms at Kensington Palace that he had reserved for his own use. When the Duchess arrived on the day before the party it was noticed that the King warmly welcomed Princess Victoria but that he gave her mother the most frigid of receptions. In the course of the following day William brooded on the Duchess's iniquities, and by the evening his rage had fully matured. At the end of his birthday banquet the King climaxed a long career of public indiscretion by rising before a hundred guests to deliver what was perhaps the most formidable oration of his life. 'I trust in God', he opened, 'that my life may be spared for nine months longer, after which period, in the event of my death, no Regency would take place. I should then have the satisfaction of leaving the exercise of the Royal authority to the personal authority of that young lady, heiress presumptive to the Crown, and not in the hands of a person now near me, who is surrounded by evil advisers and is herself incompetent to act with propriety in the situation in which she would be placed. I have no hesitation in saying that I have been insulted – grossly and continually insulted – by that person, but I am determined to endure no longer a course of behaviour so disrespectful to me. Amongst many other things I have particularly to complain of the manner in which that young lady has been kept away from my court . . . I would have her know that I am King and that I am determined to make my authority respected . . .'

The Duchess sat through the entire tirade in silence, but the overwrought Princess Victoria collapsed in tears. After dinner the Duchess was only with difficulty persuaded to forbear from leaving immediately, but she departed in high dudgeon the following day. That William had gone too far is undeniable. Adolphus Fitzclarence sensibly told his father that, although the Duchess's behaviour merited a private rebuke, this public chastisement was altogether excessive. And yet it is hard to avoid deriving a certain satisfaction from the Duchess's total rout. For years she had flouted good manners and good taste in her treatment of the King. Her ultimate exposure and humiliation seems no more than justice, rough indeed, but to be savoured none the less. Henceforth, relations between the two courts were to be coldly reserved, more akin to armed neutrality than open hostility.

209

Political relations in 1837 opened on a sour note. The speech from the throne drawn up by the ministers for the opening of Parliament in January contained a reference to a forthcoming measure of Irish municipal reform, a proposal to which the King strongly objected. To avoid giving the speech, William pleaded that the illness of the Duchess of Gloucester prevented him from opening Parliament in person. Such a ruse now seemed preferable to him than the strain of confronting his ministers with open defiance. On one point, however, he did show some of his old obstinacy, objecting to a proposed measure to abolish Church rates. The Government was going to press on regardless, but by June it had anyway become apparent that support in the House of Commons would be too meagre to pass the Bill that session. The ministerial majority had been dwindling too steadily to allow for the introduction of much controversial legislation. Both Government and King had lost the fire of their former years. It was this, rather than a fundamental change of attitude in either party, that accounted for the comparative quiescence of political affairs in the last year of William's reign.

At the beginning of the year a further slight decline had been perceptible in the King's health, without as yet occasioning serious alarm. In the spring, indeed, concern focused more on the condition of the Queen, who had returned from a visit to Germany very unwell. Then, in April, the King suffered a grievous blow. His gay and vivacious eldest daughter Sophia de l'Isle died a fortnight after giving birth to a child, a calamity all the more distressing for its unexpectedness. It seemed at least that the King's anguish would be partly alleviated by a reconciliation with his eldest son. On Sophia's death Lord Munster had sent his father a letter of condolence, a communication which led the King to hope that their recent estrangement would soon be terminated. He responded with a letter of almost pathetic eagerness, imploring Munster to return to him. 'However I do certainly approve generally of your conduct', he assured his son in a tremulous postscript, 'I cannot but regret you have estranged yourself from my house, and trust therefore, I shall shortly see you'. The appeal was to fall on deaf ears. Munster indicated that to pay a visit to his old and sick father before his claims had been met in full would entail a gross

preceding pages Princess Victoria visiting Brighton in 1832. To William's vexation, the Duchess of Kent insisted on taking her daughter on a progress through England even in the year of the Reform Bill, when the popular reception afforded to Victoria contrasted sadly with the King's own decline in favour, as a result of his stance on reform.

violation of his principles. In late May the despondent King was obliged to accept that further approaches to his eldest son would be entirely futile. By that time the King was already in the grip of his final illness.

In April the King had suffered a particularly severe bout of asthma, which had deprived him of sleep and sapped his strength. Despite his exhaustion, he had continued to undertake his normal duties. On 17 May he returned to Windsor after a levée in a state of virtual collapse. His breathing was restricted and he could only climb the stairs with difficulty, having to rest at the top. He paid little heed, however, holding the usual drawing-room reception the following day and even launching into a long discourse on naval history at dinner. His health could not withstand such activity: by 20 May his appetite had entirely gone and he was suffering from fainting fits. He continued to see his ministers, and on 27 May he even attended a Council Meeting in a wheelchair, but he was never to leave his private apartments again.

At least he was not too ill to appreciate the fact that on 24 May Princess Victoria attained her majority. William had hoped to celebrate her eighteenth birthday by entirely freeing her from her mother's control. He proposed that she should be given an annual grant of £10,000 and a separate privy purse managed by Sir Benjamin Stephenson, an individual for whom he knew the Duchess of Kent entertained a particular aversion. Although William took the precaution of ensuring that the letter was delivered to Victoria herself, he could not prevent the Duchess and Conroy from pressuring the Princess into signing a reply insisting that she wished for no change in the administration of her affairs. 'Victoria did not write that letter', the King growled perceptively when he saw its contents. The financial arrangements for the Princess were never settled to the King's satisfaction. He did, however, at least have the pleasure of knowing that the hated Duchess of Kent could never now be Regent.

Meanwhile the King's condition had continued to deteriorate. No public indication was at first given of his failing health. The usual house party assembled for Ascot in early June, although William was unable to entertain his guests and the Queen was obliged to attend the races without him. However,

on 8 June the visitors were sent home prematurely, and the following day a guarded announcement was issued admitting that the King was suffering from 'an affection of the chest'. The King's growing weakness, occasioned by his lack of sleep, coughing fits, difficulty in breathing and poor circulation ensured that a plan to transfer him to the bracing air of Brighton had to be abandoned. In the ensuing week he occasionally benefited from interludes of restfulness, but of his full recovery there seemed little hope. His main organs were ceasing to function properly: it was later discovered that the valves of his heart had hardened and his liver was swollen. On 15 June Melbourne informed the Cabinet that the Queen wished for her husband's health to be prayed for in the churches. 'It is very doubtful whether the King will survive long, but the order may as well be given', he commented cynically, his thoughts already turning to arrangements for the accession of a new monarch. At Kensington Palace Princess Victoria awaited William's death with dutiful composure, for the death of an uncle that in truth she hardly knew could not really move her. 'The news of the King are so very bad that all my lessons save the Dean's are put off', she confided to her diary on 15 June. 'I regret rather my singing lesson, though it is only for a short period, but duty and *proper feeling go before all pleasures.*' At Windsor, meanwhile, the prolonged drama went on. As the King's life slowly ebbed away he derived much comfort from religion. On one occasion Queen Adelaide hesitatingly enquired if William would like her to read him some prayers. 'Oh, Yes! Beyond everything', came the eager reply. Augustus Fitzclarence for once behaved with becoming Christian charity, reading his father selections from the Prayer Book. The 18 June was the anniversary of the Battle of Waterloo, a glorious date very dear to the patriotic old King's heart. Some days before, he had told Dr Chambers, 'Doctor, I know I am going, but I should like to see another anniversary of the Battle of Waterloo. Try if you cannot to tinker me up to last out that day.' Wellington sent to enquire if, in view of the King's condition, he should cancel the traditional dinner commemorating the battle. William would not hear of it. Grasping for the last time the folds of a small tricolour flag captured at Waterloo, the King murmured benignly, 'Tell the Duke of Wellington that I desire his dinner may take place

preceding pages Kensington Palace, where Princess Victoria lived with her mother. William hoped that the Princess could have a separate establishment on attaining her majority in order to free her from the pernicious influence of the Duchess of Kent.

tomorrow. I hope it may be an agreeable one.' As the preparations to celebrate the anniversary went ahead, William was taking the sacrament for the last time. The Archbishop of Canterbury had come to see him on the morning of 18 June, and administered communion to the King, and to Adelaide and Lady Mary Fox. The following day he returned to read the service for the visitation of the sick. When he came to the blessing the strain on the Queen, who had been in such constant attendance over the past ten days that she had not even had time to change her clothes, became too much, and she burst into tears. 'Bear up, bear up', said the King in gruff consolation. By now it was clear that William's life was fast drawing to a close. With the exception of Munster, his children assembled in his room for a final blessing. As the evening progressed he became steadily weaker, occasionally losing consciousness altogether. At twelve minutes past two on the morning of 20 June 1837, the last fitful spark of life was finally extinguished.

'Poor man, he was always very kind to me and he *meant* it well I know', recorded Victoria at Kensington, about to start on her momentous reign; 'I am grateful for it and shall ever remember his kindness with gratitude. He was odd, very odd, and singular, but his intentions were often ill-interpreted.' She owed the King more perhaps than she realized. When William IV ascended the throne the monarchy was sickly and in decline. When he died, a mere seven years later, it was a flourishing institution. Miss Wynne, a contemporary diarist, noted the contrast between the sorrow which greeted the news of William's death and the indifference which met his brother's. 'Then few, very few, thought it necessary to assume the mask of grief; *now* one feeling seems to actuate the nation! Party is forgotten and all mourn . . .' It was fitting tribute for one who had always striven for a consensus between moderate men of good sense. The King had believed it his function not to oppose all change but to mediate between conflicting passions so that change could be achieved without destruction. His own prejudices were considerations entirely secondary to the performance of his duty. It was William IV, rather than his father or brother, who took the monarchy into the nineteenth century. By doing so he contributed to its continued existence in the twentieth.

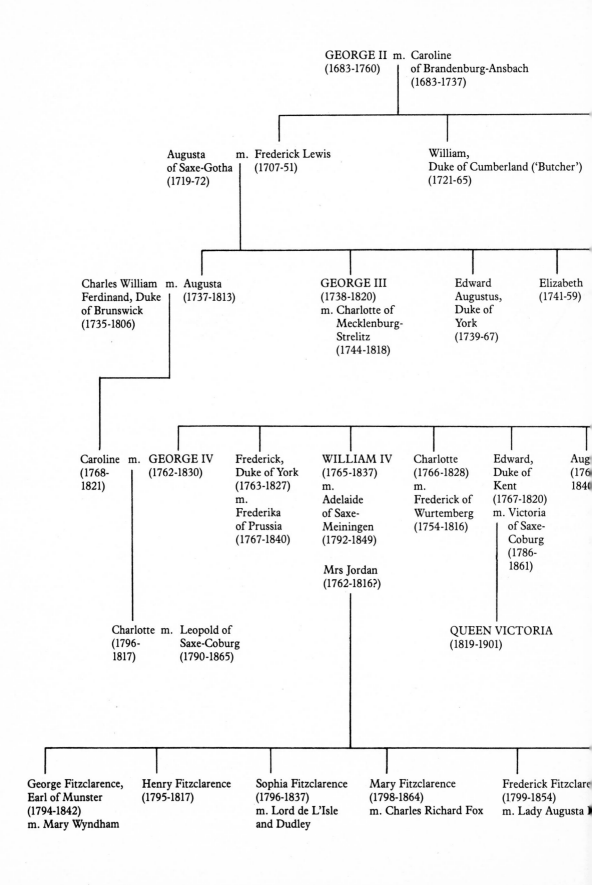

GEORGE II m. Caroline
(1683-1760)   of Brandenburg-Ansbach
  (1683-1737)

Augusta   m.   Frederick Lewis
of Saxe-Gotha   (1707-51)
(1719-72)

William,
Duke of Cumberland ('Butcher')
(1721-65)

Charles William   m.   Augusta
Ferdinand, Duke   (1737-1813)
of Brunswick
(1735-1806)

GEORGE III
(1738-1820)
m. Charlotte of
  Mecklenburg-
  Strelitz
  (1744-1818)

Edward
Augustus,
Duke of
York
(1739-67)

Elizabeth
(1741-59)

Caroline   m.   GEORGE IV
(1768-   (1762-1830)
1821)

Frederick,
Duke of York
(1763-1827)
m.
Frederika
of Prussia
(1767-1840)

WILLIAM IV
(1765-1837)
m.
Adelaide
of Saxe-
Meiningen
(1792-1849)

Mrs Jordan
(1762-1816?)

Charlotte
(1766-1828)
m.
Frederick of
Wurtemberg
(1754-1816)

Edward,
Duke of
Kent
(1767-1820)
m. Victoria
of Saxe-
Coburg
(1786-
1861)

Aug
(176
184(

Charlotte   m.   Leopold of
(1796-   Saxe-Coburg
1817)   (1790-1865)

QUEEN VICTORIA
(1819-1901)

George Fitzclarence,
Earl of Munster
(1794-1842)
m. Mary Wyndham

Henry Fitzclarence
(1795-1817)

Sophia Fitzclarence
(1796-1837)
m. Lord de L'Isle
and Dudley

Mary Fitzclarence
(1798-1864)
m. Charles Richard Fox

Frederick Fitzclar
(1799-1854)
m. Lady Augusta

HOUSE OF HANOVER

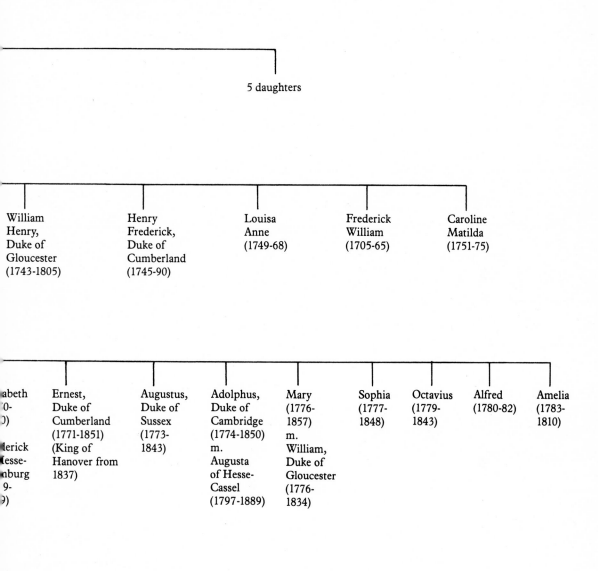

5 daughters

William
Henry,
Duke of
Gloucester
(1743-1805)

Henry
Frederick,
Duke of
Cumberland
(1745-90)

Louisa
Anne
(1749-68)

Frederick
William
(1705-65)

Caroline
Matilda
(1751-75)

abeth
0-
0)

Ernest,
Duke of
Cumberland
(1771-1851)
(King of
Hanover from
1837)

Augustus,
Duke of
Sussex
(1773-
1843)

Adolphus,
Duke of
Cambridge
(1774-1850)
m.
Augusta
of Hesse-
Cassel
(1797-1889)

Mary
(1776-
1857)
m.
William,
Duke of
Gloucester
(1776-
1834)

Sophia
(1777-
1848)

Octavius
(1779-
1843)

Alfred
(1780-82)

Amelia
(1783-
1810)

lerick
lesse-
nburg
9-
9)

beth Fitzclarence
-1856)
ord Erroll

Adolphus Fitzclarence
(1802-1856)

Augusta Fitzclarence
(1803-1865)
m. (i) John Erskine
   (ii) Lord Fred Gordon

Augustus Fitzclarence
(1805-1854)
m. Sarah Gordon

Amelia Fitzclarence
(1807-1858)
m. Lord Falkland

Select bibliography

Aspinall, A. (ed.), *The Later Correspondence of George III*, Cambridge University Press (1962–7)

Aspinall, A. (ed.), *Correspondence of George, Prince of Wales*, Cassell, London (1963–70)

Aspinall, A. (ed.), *The Letters of George IV*, Cambridge University Press (1938)

Aspinall, A. (ed.), *Mrs Jordan and her Family*, Arthur Barker Ltd, London (1951)

Aspinall, A. (ed.), *Three Early Nineteenth-Century Diaries*, Williams and Norgate, London (1952)

Briggs, Asa, *The Age of Improvement*, Longman, Green, London (1959)

Brock, Michael, *The Great Reform Act*, Hutchinson University Library, London (1973)

Butler, J. R. M., *The Passing of the Great Reform Bill*, Longman, Green, London (1914)

Cecil, David, *Lord M.*, Constable, London (1954)

Fothergill, Brian, *Mrs Jordan*, Faber & Faber, London (1965)

Fulford, Roger, *Royal Dukes*, Duckworth, London (1933)

Fulford, Roger, *From Hanover to Windsor*, Batsford, London (1960)

Gash, Norman, *Peel*, Longman, Green, London, (1976)

Hibbert, Christopher, *George IV*, vols I and II, Longman, Green, London (1972, 1973)

Hopkirk, Mary, *Queen Adelaide*, John Murray, London (1946)

Longford, Elizabeth, *Victoria R.I.*, Weidenfeld & Nicolson, London (1964)

Longford, Elizabeth, *Wellington, Pillar of State*, Weidenfeld & Nicolson, London (1972)

Ridley, Jasper, *Palmerston*, Constable, London (1970)

Sandars, Mary, *Queen Adelaide*, Stanley Paul, London (1915)

Trevelyan, G. M., *Lord Grey of the Reform Bill*, Longman, Green, London (1915)

Turberville, A. S., *The House of Lords in the Age of Reform*, Faber & Faber, London (1958)

Walder, Alan David, *Nelson*, Hamish Hamilton, London (1978)

Watson, Stephen, *The Reign of George III*, Oxford University Press (1960)

Ziegler, Philip, *William IV*, William Collins, London (1971)

Ziegler, Philip, *Melbourne*, William Collins, London (1976)

Index